Live Life with Ease

Everyday Paths to Self-Worth

Harish Malhotra

ISBN-10: 0692575251
ISBN-13: 978-0692575253

Published by Partners in Psychiatry Press (PiPP)
www.PartnersInPsychiatry.com

Edited & Prepared for Publication by Jennifer-Crystal Johnson
www.JenniferCrystalJohnson.com

Book Cover Image:
"Converse Fields" by Ilham Rahmansyah
https://commons.wikimedia.org/wiki/File:ConverseFields(byIlhamRahmansyah).jpg

Book Cover Design & Layout by Jennifer-Crystal Johnson

Table of Contents

Introduction

The patient looked down as he said, "I cannot solve my problems. I feel hopeless. I don't want to live anymore."

I replied, "Suicide is a problem-solving behavior. People think of suicide as the last way of solving a problem when they think that problems are unsolvable. I can understand why you are thinking of suicide."

He looked up at me but didn't say anything.

I continued, "Make believe that your house has termites. You have already used chemical sprays, but the termites are still thriving. Would you set your house on fire to get rid of the termites?"

The patient looked at me in disbelief. "No, I would not."

Once I got his attention, I asked, "What would you do instead?"

The patient thought for a moment and said, "Get a termite specialist."

I said with enthusiasm, "Correct. You got it right. If you burn the house down, you will kill the termites as well as destroy your house. Similarly, if you kill yourself, you will not only stop the problem, but you will also stop yourself from living."

The use of the termite metaphor helped the patient understand the unproductive nature of the act of suicide. He also agreed to work with me in psychotherapy to find solutions to his problems. I have used the 'house with termites' story with many patients to engage them in further dialog.

In the beginning, I doubted what I was writing. However, as I started researching on the internet, I found that there were books containing metaphors and websites with metaphoric cartoons. The discovery strengthened my resolve to share my collection. My patients have mentioned the positive role the stories played in their lives. Given this favorable development, I was encouraged to create and use new metaphors in my practice. I documented each one until I had a sufficient amount for a book.

My family and I made funny short videos and posted them on YouTube. We named them Helpful Hints for Hang-ups. People liked the simplicity of the messages and my first book, *Metaphors of Healing*, was born.

The fun little things did proved to be life-changing for me. Patients and colleagues alike sincerely appreciated my efforts, and I was inspired to publish my second book, *Pathways to Hope*.

Previously, I used the stories with hesitation to communicate insights to my patients. As time passed, I used metaphors more assertively in cognitive behavior therapy, putting some level of trust in the technique. Outside of the physician-patient sphere, my family and I have become so sensitive to their use that we appreciate each other coming up with new ones.

I attended seminars on dialectic behavior therapy and felt encouraged that metaphors are a common element of the treatment. I observed how mental health professionals used metaphors in therapy. I watched highly successful colleagues in psychoanalysis and cognitive behavior therapy. I marveled at the fact that the most effective moments of their sessions were when they used a metaphor.

Colleagues in my field have embraced my books. Both of these books have become self-help resources for my patients and the general population alike. People have bought the books and sent them to their family and friends as gifts. I have some patients who carry the books with them to read whenever they get some spare time.

The New Jersey Psychiatric Association awarded me the Exceptional Achievement Award because of *Metaphors of Healing*. I was also the recipient of the Physicians Excellence Award from the Overlook Hospital in Summit, NJ. Part of the credit was due to the two books I had written.

It would give me great joy if my third book, *Live Life with Ease: Everyday Paths to Self-Worth* proves helpful. Please use the wisdom of these metaphors for your clients, patients, and yourselves. They are self-help books to repair potholes in your everyday paths.

Acknowledgments

Many people shaped my life and helped me put my heart and soul into this book.

My laughing, crying, dancing, and creativity came from my mother, Mrs. Krishna Malhotra. My father, Mr. Sohan Lal, was a silent pillar in our family. He modeled how to be a man through his actions. My brother, Satish, has been a symbol of integrity all my life.

Kirpa Devi, my paternal grandmother, kept busy without focusing on her limitations. She took away my fear of death.

My aunt, Janak Beeji, kept her family together like glue for as long as she could. Cousin Satinder's loving and generous heart spilled over with love for all, including me. Cousin Jatinder would not take BS from anyone. My nephew, Vishu, meets everybody with a radiant smile, even for the first time.

My maternal Uncle Pali Mama's love for his nephews and nieces taught me to become a loving uncle.

My Aunt Prakash Vati's family – Yashpal, Anand, and Kiran – changed me from a faith-based person to a logic-based person early in life.

Aunt Bimla loved people in the gentlest manner. Uncle Gian Chand Khanna's presence was like shade from the bright sunshine, making people feel good in the oppressive heat of life.

Cousin Pushpa came from a very difficult place in life with a poor support system. But she became a physician in America, paving the way for the rest of the clan.

My eldest son, Gautam, has the honesty of making decisions based on his gut feelings. My daughter-in-law, Monica, has a soul of steel and the gentle heart of a mother of two angels, Kavina and Athena.

Rahul, my younger son, is an exceptional student and has made me less intellectually lazy. "If you do not know a fact, search on the internet," he says.

My parents-in-law, Bharat and Manorma Khanna, were wise people. Mummy never criticized me or took sides in our marital squabbles.

Hakeem Saheb, a Muslim elderly gentleman, conversed with me as if I were an adult when I was in 9th grade. "Shukria!" to Hakeem Saheb, wherever you are.

My biology teacher, whose name I cannot recall, made the impossible possible by teaching me to study 16 hours in a day.

The above-mentioned seeds were planted in me all my life. They are still blooming within.

A thousand kisses to my wife, Mahamaya. She is a friend, partner, advisor, and a lover all rolled into one. She fills my life with her gentle voice and silky touch.

Salman Akhtar is a dear friend. I have liked and loved him since 1968. He has filled my life with closeness, guidance, laughter, and sweetness.

Vinay Kumar taught me that you can rise as high as you want to and still keep your feet on the ground.

Madho Sharma is a God-sent friend, physician, and healer who saved my life. I saw large hands firmly holding a little child. That was how I visualized us when he took charge of my illness from June 2012. Thanks to Dr. Michael Nissenblatt for keeping me alive with tender doctoring.

Finally, I would like to thank my loved ones for looking up to me as their 'pillar of the family.' This is an honor that has given me additional reason to live.

I want to thank Clemencia Amor Neri for making sense out of my nonsensical dictations and fine-tuning the writing until it was ready to be edited by Ms. Jennifer-Crystal Johnson, who has done a great job with my books.

Most of all, thanks to my readers for your appreciation.

Harish Malhotra, MD

Chapter 1:
Every Problem Has a Solution

Are You Stuck in Your Ways?

We are used to doing things a certain way. Oftentimes, we feel disabled when our familiar methods are not available. For example, someone who has lost a limb, money, their house, or their spouse may not be able to see themselves living life anymore. They are like someone who always travels on a certain highway. The moment that road is closed, he might believe that he cannot make it to his destination.

The good news is that this is not a problem to someone who uses other roads from time to time. Someone who does would immediately think of those alternate routes when the highway situation changes.

When your circumstances change, don't handle it in a fixed way. Tell yourself, "Others do things differently. There is a way for me to do this. I will find new ways of solving my problems."

Rise Above Your Limitations

I lost my eyeglasses, so I searched my home, my car, and my office to no avail.

How will I check my emails? I thought. I was frustrated, thinking that my whole evening was going to be wasted.

Then another thought came.

I use eyeglasses to enlarge what I'm reading. What if I use my computer's capability to enlarge type on the screen?

I located the zoom button and was able to use the internet. I found an alternative method to defeat the limitations of my eyesight.

9

We are aware of our limits in regard to finances, time, and relationships. We tend to look at their status as 'fixed,' but there are always solutions.

Be firm and counter your insecurity with the knowledge that there are many ways to solve your problems. Find out what they are.

Kicking Tires

A car was traveling smoothly on the highway.

Bang! It swerved, then stopped. The driver exited the car to check what happened.

A flat tire!

He had three options:

1. Get back in the car and sulk.
2. Curse, kick the tire, and hurt his foot.
3. Get help or change the tire himself.

The first is the typical response of most people in a crisis. They succumb to paralysis, not knowing what to do. The second response is annoyance, impatience, and yelling. For them, it is the fault of others, and those people must be punished.

Take step number three.

Ask yourself: "Am I fixing the car or am I only injuring my foot? Am I taking steps to straighten out my situation, or am I just ruffled and rattled? Am I taking concrete steps to solve this problem?"

If you have AAA or your insurance covers roadside assistance, give them a call. If you know how to change your tire yourself, do so. Find the solution that is safe and practical for you.

Chapter 2:
Switch Off the Stress Button

The Place, a Place, Someplace

The place is a spot in your house that you have designated to put your car keys, wallet, eyeglasses, loose change, and handkerchiefs. *A place* is a spot in the house where you leave things because you are in a rush. *Someplace* is a spot in the house where you put stuff and totally forget about it.

This is what often happens with elderly people. We say, "I put my eyeglasses *someplace,* but I cannot recall where."

Stress fills our lives; we should not add to it. Misplacing eyeglasses, keys, and cell phones creates extra stress. We cannot see things clearly; we cannot unlock our car, desk drawers, cabinets, or rooms; we cannot access the phone numbers and addresses stored in our phones.

Many stressors are not under our control because they are unpredictable. But one thing is: putting things in *the place* can make a difference in our daily battle against stress.

Pin-Drop or Ton-Drop

Beth gets easily upset with many things: an irate customer, a telephone call from her mother, a lost document, or a suggestion from her boss.

She ordered Japanese fried rice, but Chinese fried rice was delivered. She screamed at the delivery man. The remainder of her day was ruined. By afternoon, she was ready to bite off the heads of her colleagues.

She was unaware of her emotional reactions.

For example, a fax machine failed to function. She simply had to call the repairman. A phone call from the school nurse said that she had to collect her feverish child within the hour. She simply had to decide whether she would leave work or call her mother to pick up her child.

Confronted by these situations, she ran out of the office sobbing, "I can't take it anymore!"

A non-working fax machine is easier to handle than attending to a sick child. The fax is a pin-drop, the sick child is a ton-drop. The case of the Japanese and Chinese rice was a pin-drop. It could be easily shrugged off by being more flexible.

Do not react to pin-drops and ton-drops with the same intensity. A pin-drop warrants less emotional energy. A ton-drop needs problem-solving skills.

Let the small mishaps slide by. Save your aggravation for heavier cases.

The Doormat Needs Cleaning

Doormats are put in entryways to serve as a 'check-in counter' for dirt on people's footwear. It becomes dark, drab, and grimy. It needs to be cleaned up. You take it into the driveway and swing it against a wall, fence, or pillar. The dust and dried mud comes out, then you bring it back to its place.

Are you an attorney, an accountant, or a salesman? Do you work in a profession where you feel like you have absorbed too much of other people's dirt? Do people come to you upset, annoyed, and stressed out with their problems?

What you are experiencing is normal in your line of work. Counter it by making evenings and weekends your 'cleaning period.' Take care of the dirt stuck on you by relaxing with a game of tennis, golf, or cards, or a visit to a street fair. It does not matter what you swing against as long as the dust flies out of you. Carefully plan and enjoy your 'dusting schedule!'

The Heavy Bag

"I work seven days a week and I'm exhausted. I have no time for myself. I am angry at others who put demands on me," Stella said. She blamed her family for her stressed out condition.

"Let's suppose that you stuffed things in a bag. Who is responsible for the stuff inside your bag? Is it the owner of the stuff or you who did the stuffing?" I asked.

"I am, but they need those things done."

"People are going to ask you to do things based on *their* needs. *You* have to decide how much you can take on."

"What do you mean?"

"Decide what goes into your bag. There is no limit as to how much you put in the bag, but your back has a limit as to how much weight it can carry."

A Candle Burning at Both Ends

You go beyond your emotional and physical capacity to please others. In your excessive striving, you are like a candle burning at both ends. You have grown resentful, though it is not other people's fault.

You are like a candle that burns on one end. When the light you produce is not appreciated, you try harder, so you light the wick on the other end.

However, the life of a candle burning on both ends is quickly snuffed out. People may thank you for burning bright at first, but the contrast is noticeable when darkness fills the room after that. People may criticize you for not being available all the time.

When it comes to helping your family, friends, and career, ask, "Am I burning naturally or am I burning at both ends?" Be honest with yourself. If your reply is the latter, you are a sure candidate for burnout.

Only do what you can maintain easily and consistently. Do not give gifts or cash to your loved ones that you cannot sustain. If you feel resentful when you give, that is a red flag. Scale it down.

Burn naturally, last long. Burn on both ends, expire early.

Strain or Exercise

Lie face down on a carpet. Stretch both of your arms up at the side of your head, with both legs stretched back and your toes pointed to the floor. Lift your arms and legs slowly to two inches off the floor. This position leaves only your stomach and chest touching the floor. Keep this position to the count of 15, then let go and relax. This exercise will give your neck, shoulders, back, and legs a good stretch.

Exercising is good for the body. We know that. However, when you exercise more than your body can take, the exercise turns into a strain.

An eight-hour workday, a weekend of golf, a shopping spree, or a vacation is good for your health. But when these are done beyond their limits, they create strain on your body, bank account, and relationships.

Be careful not to overextend your work and hobbies to avoid emotional strain. Be careful not to overextend the capacity of your wallet to avoid the dollar drain.

Chapter 3:
Stop What's Stopping You

Go Ahead, Do It

"I want to do many things, but I don't think I can do them."

"I'm not good at the things I want to do."

"I don't think people will approve of the things I want to do."

Let's suppose there is a man who has an ordinary car, like a Honda. Another has a $70,000 Mercedes Benz. Would the number of miles they travel depend on the make of the car they drive or would it depend on their effort and determination to do the driving?

The car model doesn't make a difference. Interest and determination do; they are the main factors.

I know a veteran who was in a wheelchair. He traveled all over the US. He waited until somebody gave him a ride, then he would travel somewhere new and wait for another ride, and so on. He was in a wheelchair, yet he was able to visit most parts of the country.

Some people have lots of money, several cars, and time, yet they do not travel. They find reasons not to. In most cases, hindrances are not caused by outside circumstances; they are manufactured inside a person's head.

Overcome your inner blockades. In doing so, your desire will not remain a dream.

Disability Benefits: A Secure Prison Cell

Some people develop severe illnesses that preclude them from continuing their job, so they apply for disability benefits. The application is approved or denied based on the severity of their condition. As time goes on, other chronic illnesses and

15

complications are added to the burden. The patient is declared permanently disabled.

Every patient's case is subject to review every five years. He continues to get treatment for this chronic illness. Additional medical records accumulate. They prove that he is unwell; hence, the disability benefit continues.

I have seen many cases where the person improved and stabilized. In fact, if they were to educate, train, and rehabilitate themselves into a job, they could earn more than they did at their original job. As it was, the security of a regular check made them hesitate in getting out of this comfortable place.

"You have imprisoned and locked yourself into poverty," I told my patient.

"What do you mean?" he asked.

"You are getting this small check that is equal to two weeks of pay in a regular job. You deny yourself the opportunity of earning more. You have sacrificed further education and personal improvement in exchange for this 'secure prison' that is only equivalent to two meals a day and a bed to sleep on."

We Are Not Saving Enough

My wife and I started our married life as a poor couple. Then things improved. My earnings rose to $11K, to $50K, to $150K, and to $200K a year, but saving for the future remained a priority in my mind. I would tell her, "We are spending too much; we are not saving enough."

"If we keep on saving, when are we going to live and enjoy our life?" my wife would counter. But foremost in my mind was to protect my family from poverty; hence, I was dogmatic about our savings.

I had an epiphany one day. My wife and I sat down and discussed it. We agreed what percentage of our earnings should go to our monthly savings. The total amount of money we would be saving for our retirement would be the maximum amount allowed by law.

We established a clear goal, I stopped complaining, and our bickering ceased.

The word 'savings' is an unreachable dream to some people. It is like following a beautiful rainbow to see where it touches the earth. Then the person discovers that there is nothing there.

But 'savings' don't have to be like that. Sit down with your spouse and agree on concrete figures, then stick to the plan you have set. As for the rest of the money, use it for your family's maintenance and leisure.

Onward to peace with family finances!

Become a Fly Swatter

Joey complained that opportunities were slippery. He had job interviews, but nothing went beyond that. All he did over the course of six months was lie on the couch, watch TV, and curse his situation.

During one of my visits to his house, I noticed something: he had a fly swatter beside him. He was alert and fast. A fly was as good as dead inside his home.

"Treat your job hunting the same as your fly swatting," I urged him. "You hit flies because you get up to your feet fast and go after them with all your might.

"Opportunities are like flies. They quickly come and go. Get out of your house. Be watchful for opportunities. When you see one, give it your best attack with a 'job swatter' until you catch a job."

Chapter 4:
The Efficacy of Writing Things Down

Restless Nights

You have regularly interrupted sleep. You always wake up in the middle of the night.

What for?

To solve a problem.

If you recall, you didn't actually solve the problem by tossing and turning in bed. If you did solve the problem, it was not an earth-moving problem and solution. It wasn't worth those bags under your eyes.

What should you do about it?

Keep a notepad and pen on your night table. When a problem pops up, write it down. Tell yourself, "I have this down on paper; this problem will not slip my mind tomorrow. I am getting my sleep now."

Every time the same thought crosses your mind, allow yourself to stop thinking about it because you have it written down, so you don't have to remember it.

When another problem surfaces, do the same thing. Write it down and say, "I will think about this tomorrow. I'm not messing up my sleep tonight."

In the morning, when you review what you have written, you will notice that the problems and solutions are no big deal. You can then deal with them during the day.

Refuse to occupy your sleep time with problem-solving thoughts. Put your problems on paper instead. There will be little difference at first, but when you make this a habit every time you are pestered at night, it won't be long before you sleep like a baby.

The Problems of Life

We are surrounded by all sorts of problems. They pop up every now and then, sometimes many at the same time. Some of them overwhelm us. They are like clutter in the house: papers, clothes, shoes, toys, dishes in the sink. However, the confusion disappears once we take care of them one by one.

Writing down the issues can help. Put them in separate groups. Write the smallest and easiest problems first. Then start working on the ones that you can take care of right away. These could be simple things like shampooing the carpets, answering holiday cards, or paying the bills. Take care of the difficult things last.

The Worry Wasps

Do you worry about minor things? Do they become so upsetting that you cannot hide your distraction?

Your loved ones notice and ask, "Are you worried about something?"

"No, not really," you say, shaking your head. But as soon as you finish saying it, you go back to thinking of those 'worry wasps' again.

Use the following trick: Write down your worries on a piece of paper. Put the paper on your kitchen counter and say, "Worry wasps, you are stuck on this paper! I am going to cover you with a heavy dome of lead. I will free you when I return."

Cover the paper with a wok or pot and walk away.

When a worry crosses your mind, say, "You cannot escape. You're under the massive dome in my kitchen. I cannot reach you; you cannot reach me," then refocus on your surroundings or your current task.

Isolating yourself from those worries for six hours will give your mind a break. You will be able to attend to one problem at a time. At a designated time, lift the wok. Then check what you wrote. Decide what you will do with each issue.

Should you discard a worry because it is trivial? Should you take care of a worry because it is important?

Harness Your Racing Mind

We have little control over racing thoughts. The same ideas continue to pester us. Each time they appear, we receive them and they occupy our minds over and over.

While laying down in bed, I had this jumble of thoughts in my mind. I sat up to write them on a piece of paper to sort them out and deal with them one by one.

You know what, believe it or not, I was able to write down only one sentence! No matter how I tried to make sense out of those thoughts, there was only one legitimate, clear issue. Only *one* thing had bugged me for an hour. How ridiculous!

That's what a racing mind is. A lot of stuff whirls in our mind, but once we enumerate it in writing, we realize that our mind's motor was running in neutral without covering any distance. We were repeating the same idea in different ways. It was like saying, "I want ten dollars," in 30 languages!

Don't be deceived. Write your thoughts down and see the culprit: a solo performer hiding behind a haze of jumbled shadows.

Being First on the List

You want to be first on people's list of favorite persons. You also want to be their number one priority. Anytime you find it otherwise, you feel rejected, insecure, and angry.

How can you become their top priority?

Make a list of the characteristics, habits, and attitudes that attract and pull you toward people. If you want to bring yourself to the top of people's list, start doing the things from your own list. What's good for the goose is good for the gander.

How to Stop Worrying

"There is less money coming in. What am I going to do?"

"There is no money for the mortgage. How will I pay the babysitter? How will I pay the electricity and water bills?"

"No job! No money! No electricity! No water!"

This was Simon's internal dialog.

Did you notice that he was consumed by thoughts of 'no money,' 'no this,' and, 'no that?' He was being consumed by his problems and their consequences.

Can you spot what is lacking?

A third part is missing. It's called 'solutions.'

On a piece of paper, create three columns: 'Problems,' 'Consequences,' and 'Solutions.'

In the column for 'solutions,' write whatever comes to mind. Some ideas may sound absurd or unworkable in the beginning, but they can start making sense as you ponder them.

"We have only one child; Tina could babysit for others. She can earn $300-$400 a month per child."

"I can borrow from my retirement account."

"I can ask my mom for a loan."

"I can sell or pawn my jewelry."

"I can have a garage sale."

Problems? Those are just part of life. However, most of us are burdened with worry because we forget to include 'solutions' in the picture.

Chapter 5:
Accept Changes in the Family Landscape

Two More Kids

Computer, Facebook, Twitter, Gmail, Google Drive, the internet—these things might seem to come from 'outer space' in the eyes of your parents. You know that they can be very efficient, but your parents may not listen; maybe they insist on using a paper map instead of GPS.

In your annoyance, you want to scream about their bullheadedness to their faces. You are also upset with their attitude about religion and childrearing.

Let's look at things differently. You hated the toilet when you were a kid. You pooped in diapers. You got out of your seat before dinner was over. You did not go to bed on time. How did your parents handle you?

With love and patience... with care and affection.

Look at your present situation as being blessed with 'additional' children: your mom and dad. Their changing moods are like your temper tantrums when you were a kid. Their hesitation to learn computer basics is like your resistance to sit on the potty. Their resistance to learn new things is like your difficulty in obeying their instructions when you were a child.

Every time you ate your food they would say, "That's my boy! Very good! You're a big boy now."

It's your turn today to say, "That's great, Mom! Wow! You learned to send an email. I'm so proud of you!"

In the past, they encouraged you and took pride in your achievements. It's your turn to take pride in your parents' 'baby steps' in learning technology.

Verbally express your appreciation for positive changes in their attitude. If the opportunity presents itself, do this in front of other people. It will make them feel like their child still considers them a hero.

Intense vs. Gentle Relationships

Maybe you were the 'princess' of the family when you were a kid. It was because you were the only child or the only girl, or you were sick and needed extra attention. Plenty of time and gifts were lavished on you.

In your adolescent years, you no longer received the attention that you were used to. Maybe there were health reasons, business pressures, and social demands on the family. Maybe there were also financial problems.

But you could not tolerate the lack of attention. You were used to 'high gear' attention, and you demanded high performance. The standard everyday care registered as neglect to you. You withdrew in anger and distanced yourself from your family.

Let me explain what happened.

A car moving from the left lane to the middle lane slows down its speed. However, it's not straying from its course. It's still moving and covering a lot of distance. It is still going to reach its intended destination.

The 'reduced' show of love and affection does not mean decreased love and affection. In fact, do you know what it is really telling you?

It tells you that you are growing up.

Discrepancy

Arthur's daughter was getting ready to graduate from high school, and it made him anxious. He was worried about the impending discrepancy in his life.

"She will be off to college soon. She'll find a boyfriend, get married, have children, and move on with her own life." These thoughts flooded Arthur's mind. He imagined himself and his wife relegated to the sidelines of their daughter's life.

"There will be no one to take to the gym, games, and sporting events. What will we do with so much time on our hands?" he said with a sigh.

Arthur was scared of having an 'empty nest.' Most parents of teenage daughters have this frame of mind, and other parents will follow when their nest becomes empty, too.

For many years, you have neglected your interests because your world revolved around your daughter. It's about time that you disentangle yourself from the mindset of a nest full of eggs. Don't stay frozen in the psychology and behavior of being parents. Your daughter's independence is not a thing to be anxious about.

You have a vision of your daughter's development from a teen to a grown-up. Why not also see *your* evolution as the parent of a teenager to the parent of a married woman with children of her own?

How will you fill your empty space?

Fill it with your neglected interests. You are free to fly away from the empty nest to pursue your passion and explore life.

Let Go of the Bullet

You put a bullet into the chamber, take aim at your target, and hold the gun steady.

Fire! The bullet is released.

A bullet in the air is uncontrollable. It is going to travel according to factors that are beyond man's control: its weight, the air flow, the moisture in the air (whether it's raining or not). No amount of body or facial twisting to manipulate the bullet in the air will do.

Let's see how this metaphor applies to life.

The bullet represents the child. The barrel of the gun represents the child's upbringing.

You have provided a good, quality barrel by putting her in a good school, raising her in a loving household, and instilling good morals. Once she is of age and wants to move on with life, you can no longer wield unquestioned control over her. She is like a bullet released from the barrel. Whether she is going to listen to you or not becomes *her* decision. What she will do with

25

her life is *her* call. Whatever she chooses to guide her in her journey is *her* prerogative.

Trying to restrain your child after she leaves your active supervision is like trying to regulate the direction of a bullet in the air.

You did your best in keeping the barrel from rust and maintaining its shine. These facts should comfort you. You took good aim so that the bullet hits its target. Now that the bullet is in the air, just watch where it lands.

Chapter 6:
Careful, You May Be Biased

The Double Standard

Sonya was upset. Her agitated expression was coupled with a furrowed brow.

"My cousin's son got married. She invited my sisters from Florida and Canada. I live two blocks away from her, but she didn't call me. She's retaliating against me!" she screamed.

"Retaliating?" I asked, wanting her to clarify.

"My son got married last year. The celebration was limited to only 50 people, so I didn't invite her," she explained. "Now she's taking her revenge."

I said, "You have just assumed her motive as hostile. You don't know the exact reason for your exclusion on her guest list. Her reason might be justified, in the same way that yours was. She didn't make any fuss with your decision before, so accept her decision today with grace."

We tend to practice a double standard. 'When I do it, it's okay. When you do the same thing, it's not okay.'

Watch it. Be aware of whether you're doing this, as no one likes to be on the receiving end.

Why Does She Always Do This to Me?

Wearing red-tinted glasses makes a person see things in red. Blondes are red-headed, the rainbow is red, the Incredible Hulk is red, and gorillas are red. The moment someone says, "Everything is red," it's obvious—he has his red glasses on.

When a person is in love, everything is roses and sunshine. He feels buoyant. A smile is plastered on his lips. His laughter flows like water at the slightest trigger. He feels invincible. However, rain clouds are everywhere when the relationship sours. He is hurt, angry, and bitter. People's motives are suspect. In addition, he has a standard line: "Why does she do this to me all the time?"

When *'all'* people have become unfair to you, taken advantage of you, used you, or resented you, there's no doubt that you are wearing tinted glasses. When you do, people's innocent motives are lost in your misinterpretation.

There is only one way to revert to seeing things devoid of biases. Remove your emotional red-tinted eyeglasses and stop attacking reality because of your own perception.

A Nice Meal

Jay attended a dinner where the dishes served were to his liking. However, what was laid on the table did not appeal to him because he had a fever. The food made him nauseated.

Two factors must be present for a satisfying meal: the food is appetizing and the diner has a healthy appetite.

How does this apply to relationships?

A couple came for counseling. The wife was gorgeous. She was a former model. Her husband, an accountant, had not made love to her in two years. According to him, he no longer found her physically appealing.

There was no question that his wife was physically attractive; hence, we explored the other side—his appetite. A craving for food could be destroyed by the flu. We examined what was destroying his craving for intimacy.

Are you developing an illness that is affecting your vigor? Do job-related worries consume you?

When a husband is not aware that his sexual urge is waning, he has his eyes focused on the physical flaws of his mate. He will put his partner down by criticizing her weight or a number of other things.

Remember, there are two parts of a gratifying dining experience—good food and good appetite. Do not be biased against the food and blame it; check your appetite as well.

Life is Unfair

"Life is unfair," Mario said after a car accident that cost him his foot.

"You were able to finish college. You have a job. You're not an orphan; you have a loving family. You're not living on the streets. Do these blessings make life unfair?" I asked.

Calling life unfair is like a flash of anger that causes a hungry person to sweep an enticing feast off of the table and onto the floor because they don't like one of the side dishes.

You have never complained about life before. Now that something happened, life suddenly becomes unfair. Just because you're upset, is it okay for all these blessings to be overshadowed by *one* event or problem? If life is indeed unfair, you might not be alive to complain.

Don't throw the entire dinner into the garbage if you don't like one of the side dishes.

Monologue

I know a 'non-stop talker' who dominates every conversation. He doesn't know when to stop. He laughs at his own jokes. He's oblivious to whether people are interested or bored. People elbow each other to see who gets to 'escape' from his presence first.

Do you love to monopolize conversations? Here's a test to see if you are truly an engaging conversationalist.

Stop somewhere in your discourse. Listen and observe the faces of those around you when another takes over from where you left off. Your cue that they want to hear more from you is when they look in your direction for a response. On the other hand, if others take over when you pause, it means you have done right. You have passed the ball and let the conversation flow.

Remember, people don't *only* want to listen. They desire conversations about stimulating and refreshing subjects. A conversation is far more interesting than a monologue.

Chapter 7:
Appreciate the Ordinary

Boarding a Big Ship

Some seaports can't provide easy access to large ships due to their size and shallow waters. In cases like this, large ocean vessels stay at a distance. Small boats are used to transport the passengers from ship to port and vice versa.

You had set your sights on large companies for a job. You refused to accept 'small' jobs. You were scared that it would be unfavorable for your resume.

Think about this.

First, the effect of prolonged unemployment can be frustrating. It may create marital friction due to financial hardships. Second, when did engaging in small jobs and businesses become a negative thing? Taking legitimate small jobs is not a weakness on a resume. It's much easier to explain than prolonged periods of joblessness.

The passengers needed a small boat to reach the large ship docked at a distance. A job at a small company may be your bridge to a big company.

The Phone Charger

I depended on an expensive cell phone. I was not able to use it one day because its battery was low. I had to get home first to charge it.

It happened again and again, so I decided to purchase a charging cable that cost $5. It solved my problem with my mobile phone.

Do you see the reality of this situation? This $500 phone cannot function without the $5 cable. The facility and exceptional circuitry of this invention are paralyzed without the cheap charger.

Senior executives of your company are like expensive phones. They are the 'think tanks' of the business. But is there an organization that could run smoothly without its junior employees?

Nope. It needs the ordinary workers who are the arms and legs of the CEOs.

I am grateful to my reliable charger. Lower-level employees deserve courtesy and respect, as the entire company would fall to pieces without them.

Your Ordinary Knowledge

Few people have a special fund of knowledge. Most of us have day-to-day living skills like cooking, cleaning, opening a tight bottle cap, or using WD-40.

But did you know that your ordinary experience may be special knowledge to somebody with a problem or someone who hasn't learned that skill yet?

People who were confused by the different aspects of a wedding ceremony called Mary. She has four married children, so she knows a lot about weddings. She was able to help a lot of people by answering their queries. They thanked her. Her ordinary knowledge helped a lot of people because it's special knowledge to them.

If you have an everyday experience, don't underestimate it. It may become a lifesaver to others. By recognizing this fact, you will feel confident. The confidence generated by your knowledge will embolden you to help others.

Keep Change in Your Pocket

I have a couple hundred dollars in my pocket. I also keep some small change. I need change to get soda. A hundred dollar bill is totally useless in a vending machine.

Let's translate this to friends, acquaintances, and colleagues.

Don't invest only in people who are important to your profession and your business. Don't choose only those who are okay moneywise. Include people who are like 'small change' in your life: the postman, the security guy, the parking lot attendant, or your secretary. Who knows? You may need them in some unexpected turn of events. They may prove more caring than the VIP's or the rich guys in your life.

How to Become a Rock

The highway is not made of big rocks but of small pieces of pebbles stuck together. A personality is the same. It's formed by small pebbles of actions and experiences.

Going to the supermarket and buying milk, brushing your teeth, washing your clothes, cleaning the car, cleaning the bathroom, and doing an errand for Mom are a few examples of pebbles that add up to create your consciousness. When regularly done, these small actions become you. They make up the foundation of your personality.

Small things mixed together serve as a solid foundation. Big exploits are possible when the small things have been established.

The Gift of an Ordinary Day

"Where is it?" I asked in frustration.

Misplacing something is a universal thing. I used to get impatient when I wanted something that I couldn't find like my eyeglasses, keys, or a pen.

"My day is spoiled," I growled. "Honey, I can't find my glasses. Help me."

"Don't be careless with your stuff," my spouse said with annoyance. "I'm late for school."

I looked under the furniture, inside closets, inside desk drawers, and in the pockets of my dirty laundry.

Later, I reflected on my annoyance.

"An ordinary day is part of life. It's the ordinary day of a married guy with kids. The lucky ones that live long have more ordinary days."

People who have grave illness can no longer wait for special events that are few and far between.

"I have little time left, and I'm having these stupid problems," they may impatiently say. This kind of thinking will add unhappy days to their life.

How do you bring cheer to your life?

When I couldn't find my keys, I just smiled and said, "The average life is full of ordinary days. Thanks for giving me another ordinary day to live."

A missed phone call, late pizza delivery, or a flat tire no longer bug me. I look up, smile, and say, "Thank you, time, for extending my life so I can enjoy one more ordinary day."

I usually finish it with a prayer: "Can I have more ordinary days, please?"

The Discarded Jacket

A thick, old jacket was lying in a corner in my basement. I put it away because I had other jackets in my wardrobe that were better looking.

One time, the winter was very bad. In addition to the icy snow, the day was windy. I went out to shovel the snow and I was chilled to the bones.

I remembered my discarded jacket. I went inside to find and wear it and was able to finish the job without freezing.

I kept my jackets based on fashion value, not on utility value. I didn't recognize the utility value of my discarded jacket until there was an adverse circumstance.

We have friends and relatives who have more fashion value. They host a feast now and then. They call us to grace their dinner table. They offer us exquisite dishes and expensive wines.

We also have friends and relatives who are low key people. They are just simple folks. However, when a family member is sick or hospitalized, they never hesitate to comfort us.

The warmth of their presence and help aid us in conquering the cold.

It's not a sin to enjoy sleek, trendy clothes. However, also consider the clothes that offer warmth in cold weather and coolness in hot weather. Keep a discerning eye on your friends and relatives. Who are the sleek and fashionable, good for the good times? Who are the ones who hold your hand in difficult times?

Smoothing Out the Creases

You weren't sleeping well because you needed to change the mattress. However, it was easy to smooth out the creases on the bed sheet to make yourself more comfortable.

In human relationships, large differences are like the mattress. They are major things that don't disappear with the snap of your fingers. If the source of stress is a person who you cannot kick out of your life like family members or your boss, decrease the small differences and irritants. It's like sleeping on smooth bed sheets.

You can very well work on the small differences, fully knowing that the major ones still exist. Rub off the rough edges of the relationship by saying, "Good morning," "Good evening," "How are you?" and, "Thank you." These decrease the tension between you and the person causing you stress. Let these small niceties smooth out your relationship.

What Do You Say in Difficult Times?

I developed a cataract. Everything looked distorted. It was very distracting and upsetting.

I saw every traffic light and car headlight as a set of six lights. The street lights in our town resembled florets of light. It was like Christmas time.

While waiting for my cataract operation, I was able to tolerate my imperfect vision.

How?

I would humor myself by saying, "It's Christmas time!"
Guess what? This short, simple statement made me smile, and I was less upset about my problem.

Chapter 8:
Settle Into Your Ideal Lifestyle

Use a Lower Gear

We shift to higher gears on highways, a lower gear when we go up a slope, and drive when we travel distances. For fun, we sometimes drive with the roof of our car folded back or all the windows down. Same car, different moods.

Christy was a hard-working professional. She was also a supermom at home. When she was short on money, she would work harder to earn extra and buy more things. When she wanted to have fun, she would meet with friends and attend a string of parties. She learned how to speak better by joining the Toastmasters Club. She learned how to invest money by attending financial and other relevant trainings. Christy drove her life's car in overdrive.

She felt exhausted as the years went by. She expected some return, but there was nothing. She felt cheated by her friends, children, and spouse.

She scrutinized her life one day and the lightbulb finally came on: overdrive was no longer effective. Her tank was near empty.

She decided to use that remaining energy to her benefit. She cut down on activities, hobbies, and people. Her grown-up children had already moved out, so she sold her six-bedroom house to live in a three-bedroom condominium. She retained her full-time job but left her side job. She became selective in choosing friends. She moved from parties for 50 people to quiet evenings with a few people. She used to do high-impact exercises, but she switched to yoga.

If your car is getting old, of course you cannot stop your journey. However, you can shift gears and change your style of driving.

Are You a Turtle or a Fish?

I was waiting for my turn in the barber shop and the fish tank caught my attention. There was a turtle and several fish in there. I watched for about five minutes.

Within those minutes, the turtle sat like a motionless statue while the fish swam from one side of the tank to the other, stopping for only a second or two.

The two creatures' lifestyles are different. The turtles have little activity, and the fish are very mobile.

What lifestyle do you think is right? The turtle's or the fish's?

There are people who limit their socialization and activities. They are not a burden to others. They are happy and satisfied being in their own company. That is who they are.

There are also people who are always on the go. They are involved in their job, their hobbies, and their projects at home. Their phone line is busy. Their social media activity is full. That is who they are.

Any lifestyle is okay as long as it fits you and doesn't hurt the people around you.

If the turtle tried to be mobile, it would be in trouble. Why? Its body is not made to swim non-stop.

If the fish tried to be immobile, they wouldn't survive, either. Why? Their bodies are not made to be still.

Recognize who you are. Are you a fish or a turtle?

As long as you are happy, it's okay. There is no perfect way to live this life.

Phillips vs. Flathead Screwdriver

When someone is injured, he may experience difficulty in carrying out the things he was used to doing.

My patient lost the pinky finger on his right hand in an industrial accident. Prior to this, he used to play golf. After the accident, he ceased participating in the game.

"You cut down your playing, then you finally stopped. Why?"

"I was frustrated. I couldn't firmly grip the club like I did before."

"The screws on the thing you want to dismantle need a flathead screwdriver. What is available to you is a Phillips-head screwdriver. What do you do?"

"I would look for a flathead screwdriver."

"Meaning?"

"I can do the job using a flathead screwdriver."

"That's right. You do it with a different type of tool that matches the screws. In the same way, stop saying, 'I can no longer play golf as I used to.' Shift to a good, new mental tool like, 'I can play golf in a manner suited to what is available to me.' You have not lost five fingers, but one. You have not lost a hand, but a finger."

Are You the Setting Sun?

The sun has three phases.

One: its pinkish glow softly cracks through the earth's atmosphere at dawn.

Two: it turns into a super heat-giving heavenly body at noon. It burns brighter. It does not care whether it causes sunburn or heat strokes.

Three: it is time for it to set. The atmosphere becomes cool. A burst of different shades kiss the clouds. It stirs our innermost being to capture its beauty on canvas or in a song or poem.

Humans are also like the sun. When a baby is born, he becomes the apple of everyone's eyes in the family. His cuteness and his great promise in life captivate everyone.

The child grows into a confident young man. Among other things, youth is synonymous with vigor and the strength of his dreams. Oftentimes, he does not care whether he crushes others on his way to his vision.

Then maturity comes. Most often, it is accompanied by wisdom and humility. He becomes kinder. He starts shaking hands with people who are not fortunate in life. The beautiful colors of a loving spouse, a wise parent, a concerned family member, and a good citizen are pronounced. Examples are Warren Buffett and Bill and Melinda Gates. They have outpoured their money to those who are less fortunate in the world.

Where are you in your life? Are you still rising in the sky? Are you a fireball? Are you a setting sun that is spreading your colors in the sky, lifting people's spirits and cooling their world?

Chapter 9:
Learn and Expand Your Mind

Free Samples

Have you experienced this?

You went to the supermarket to shop. You saw a woman who was giving samples of chicken salad on small crackers. You knew that you were not going to buy any, but you walked over and pretended to be interested. You received a free sample.

You were still hungry, so when you saw that another woman had relieved the sales clerk, you made another round and received another sample.

You had a mini lunch of four crackers. It made you feel bright and smart. It was kind of a 'high' feeling when you got away with something without paying for it.

Education is expensive these days, and committing time is very difficult. However, your desire to gain additional knowledge is strong.

Google leads you to plenty of sites. YouTube leads you to plenty of tutorial videos. Ask.com answers your questions. These three sites give you crackers that will fulfill your appetite for learning. You will gain enough knowledge to take care of your immediate need without spending money on it.

Go to the computer for a free mini 'mind lunch.' If you are starving for knowledge, grab the free samples.

People who are knowledgeable about many things know that an unexplored unknown exists. Big areas of knowledge are still invisible and unheard of at present, just waiting to be uncovered.

The more knowledgeable you become, the more you recognize how ignorant you are about the vast number of things in the universe.

Ignorance is the Spring of Knowledge

Intelligent, knowledgeable people *know* that they don't know everything.

For example, I Googled 'India.' There was so much knowledge that I have dug up about her. I was surprised how rich the culture of my native land was. The more I learned, the more I realized how ignorant I was about my country of birth.

What areas of knowledge could you explore simply by using Google? There's a lot to be learned online for free, so if you have a desire to learn, the computer is a great place to start.

Learn from Others' Mistakes

I came to the US with my wife in 1973. Like every immigrant, I missed my family in my country of origin. My friends, who were also immigrants in the US, had conflicting thoughts about returning.

My wife and I finally made the move in 1984. We sold our house and flew to India.

We stayed in New Delhi for two years. We had difficulty with water, electricity, cockroaches, and lizards. Excessive bribery and corruption in the government were too much for us.

We came back to the USA in 1986.

Our friends were very upset when we left, thinking that they made a mistake in staying behind. When we came back, our friends got their answer. It was finally settled: staying put in the USA was the best thing.

It's not necessary to make mistakes in life, whether it's drinking alcohol, smoking cigarettes, or having an affair. The consequences of other people's decisions are more than enough to open our eyes. We can learn without paying the price ourselves.

Look at your life. What insights and wisdom have you gleaned from the victories and failures of people around you? Get your answers.

Learn from People More Successful Than You Are

A child learns to walk by holding the hands of his parents.

Man conquered the South and North Poles and Mt. Everest. Then ordinary people started doing impossible things, too. Recently, I heard that a blind person had scaled Mt. Everest.

Are you having difficulty doing something? Google it. Search to find out who has done it. If you are in the car business, study an icon like Lee Iacocca. He turned the financially crippled Chrysler Company around. If you are into computer software, look up Bill Gates.

You will find that these giants came from the same place where you are today: the beginning.

Chapter 10:
Tapping Into Your Creativity

Unleash Your Creativity

You wanted to write, paint, sculpt, and knit. However, you postponed it every time you wanted to do it. Let me offer you a story.

There are two kinds of existence for a horse.

First, there is the lifestyle of a racehorse. He wears blinders on both sides of his eyes; thus, he sees nothing but the racetrack and the finish line. He hears no voice but his master's. He aims for nothing but to be the fastest in every race.

Second, there is the lifestyle of a horse on a farm. It grazes and jumps through meadows. It neighs and snorts. It has no blinders, so it has a wide view of the scenery. This horse is free.

Being creative is being free. Creative juices flow freely when worries do not shackle the mind. First, whenever you feel like writing, painting, or sketching, do not postpone. Follow the urge without delay, otherwise it will be stifled by other things that demand your attention.

The internet is the most potent distraction there is. When you are feeding your mind with emails, Facebook, Twitter, and YouTube, it's like kicking your creativity into the storage room. When you're done, your creative urge is gone, drowned by the massive input.

Here is an additional point: competition stresses and imprisons the mind.

Avoid distraction. Avoid competition. Let your mind wander freely like the horse in the field.

Great When Alone, Great With Others

Eggs are great when you eat them hard boiled, soft boiled, scrambled, or fried. They are complete in themselves. They

45

become an omelet when you add ham, onion, or cheese. Eggs are added to help the ingredients in pastries and cakes stick together. They stay in the background and help enhance the flavor of other ingredients.

You can learn from an egg. You can be complete in yourself. You can enjoy your own company while engaging in your hobbies. You can also be warmly welcoming of your loved ones, relatives, and friends. You can enhance their lives through your positive attitude, life skills, wisdom, and talent, and vice versa.

In work-related situations, you can strengthen the organization by contributing your talent, abilities, and skills. You are like an egg in a recipe.

Remember, you have the intelligence and competence to thrive alone or in combination with others.

Why?

You are a good egg!

Make Sense Out of Nonsense

Your friend was worried, upset, and overwhelmed with problems. Do you remember the times when he came to talk to you? You talked sense into his head, right? By the time he left after an hour of chatting and sharing, he felt better. He was so grateful that when he reached home, he called you to say, "Thank you again for your help."

If you have made sense out of other people's nonsense, you can extend the same service to yourself. You have it in you.

When you are in trouble, ask yourself, "What is my problem? Am I helping myself or worsening my problem?"

You have the ability to make sense of that nonsense in your head.

Weak Back, Strong Mind

My patient, Donald, was the caretaker of a golf course. He had been taking part in physical activities and games since childhood, so his heavy manual work on the golf course was piece of cake. One day, he injured himself on the job.

"I can't do anything now. Everything I did involved a strong back. Now that my back is injured, I'm no good anymore," he said.

"Donald, don't focus on your injured back. Use your uninjured body parts and faculties," I encouraged.

It took a while to sink in. As time went by, he started to reassign his physical energies to his mind. Today, he is supervising a crew that does the physical stuff.

He said with a satisfied smile, "My back was strong and my mind was weak in the past. Today, my back is weak but my mind is strong."

Chapter 11:
Children and Their Parents

Role Modeling

"Toofy! Go to the lawn and potty!" I commanded my dog while standing on the deck one night.

Toofy did not budge. He simply looked at the surrounding darkness without moving. I took my flashlight and shone it on the lawn.

"Go, Toofy! Go potty," I repeated. Toofy remained motionless.

I did not want to wait long, so I went down the stairs myself and stood on the lawn. The dog quickly jumped to follow me, took care of his business, and ran back into the house.

What I did is called modeling. My actions told Toofy what to do. He saw that it was safe to go into the darkness because I did it myself. He was encouraged to deal with his fears.

You are a model for your children.

"Don't smoke," you told your son; but if he sees you smoking, it will confuse him. He will wonder what's wrong with smoking when you're doing it so well.

Same thing is true with drinking, uncontrolled spending, yelling, or divorcing. Giving a lecture like, "What I'm doing is bad and I am suffering. I don't want you to suffer like me," will confuse them.

If you want the dog to go to the lawn, go to the lawn yourself. If you don't want your children to smoke or drink, quit the habit.

Learning From Mom and Dad

It is common knowledge and a solid truth: children imitate their parents' behavior knowingly or unknowingly. They reflect their parents' mannerisms in talking, volume of voice, and the words being used... even yelling or screaming. Early signs of being physically violent may also surface. In short, the road map traveled by parents is a strong influence on a child's journey in life.

Do you withhold your child's toy if he doesn't get to bed on time? He would learn to go to bed in time, but you also taught him that denial is a way of relating to him.

Are you stubborn in negotiating with your child? If you are, you're going to see an obstinate adolescent, a headstrong teenager, and a pigheaded adult.

Your style of upbringing will come back to you. They may withhold their visits and affection if you disagree with them.

Remember, children grow up to be physically strong adults while parents shrink with time. So, while they are still at a 'trainable' age, teach and discipline them the way you want them to handle and deal with you when you are old and in need of their care, so watch your behavior while they're young.

Great Kids

"Go to bed at 8:00 PM."

"Chew with your mouth closed."

"Wash your hands with soap and water."

These are some of the physical instructions parents use to shape their children's habits and values.

As children are growing, they can benefit from parental guidance. They get used to receiving instructions. A child won't put a toy into his pocket because his parents teach him, "Pay before you take things from the store."

Values and personality formation take place when parents impose physical boundaries of discipline. These instructions become part of them as they are growing. It brings a sense of responsibility, honesty, righteousness, and morality, values that make for successful living.

Chapter 12:
Be Yourself and Shine!

Be a Pita, Not a Panini

At an eatery, I inquired which food displayed was a Panini. The counter clerk pointed at some bread with stuffing inside. My appetite was not stirred. I just passed by.

I saw a sign on the next counter for 'Stuffed Pita.' I saw several pieces of pita bread tucked neatly in a row. Its middle section was sliced open and stuffed with pieces of chicken, fish, roast beef, onions, and herbs. They were displayed in such a way that their fillings were showcased. They looked absolutely delicious and were difficult to resist.

I ordered one. I ate and enjoyed my pita and realized that I'd chosen it because I saw its fillings. Its insides were visible to me and made my mouth water.

There are pita and Panini people, too.

The pita person is an open book. She shares her experiences. She's not afraid to let others know her stand on issues. She is open about her convictions. She's candid about her preferences. You know her favorite places and people, and books that she is fond of. You know her as a wife, a daughter, an employee, and a friend. Her 'insides' can be seen, but they are not messily all over the place.

On the other hand, when the Panini person is at a party, she stays quiet in a corner. Though she has an opportunity to meet people, she remains closed as a cabinet. Her assumptions of rejection and negative results block her from opening up. It makes her seem boring and bland like the pressed Panini bread.

Share Your Achievements

John received commendations at a state assembly, honoring his contributions in the field of medicine. I never knew about it, though we were close buddies. He would just sit quietly while his colleagues were huddled up discussing their accomplishments.

John is a tall, handsome man who is chief of a unit in his hospital. He had a car accident during childhood that gave him a scar on his face. He became self-conscious about it. He wanted to stay unnoticed.

"John, why didn't you tell me the good news?" I complained.

"I don't like to brag," he replied.

"Sharing is not bragging," I countered. "I consider your triumph as mine because you're my friend. Please allow your friends to be happy for you. Grow and glow in our celebration of your success.

"When a relative or a close friend is in jail for a crime, we are embarrassed. When we have an achiever of a friend, we take pride in him," I continued.

"I think you're right. I did feel proud of my friend who recently wrote a book. I'll share the good news with you next time," he promised.

The Sun and the Cloud

The sun is powerful, but its heat can be intercepted. Its light can always be blocked by dark clouds, and the area below fails to receive its warmth.

In the dyads of human relationships – husband and wife, brother and sister, friends, father and son, mother and daughter – one partner may block the other's personality. He can eclipse – intentionally or unintentionally – the other person to the point that she becomes non-existent to others.

A couple frequently attended our parties. The husband would make everyone laugh with his jokes. The wife would just smile and keep quiet.

I surmised that she was reserved and didn't like to talk.

On one occasion, the wife came alone. I was amazed to discover that she was smart, knowledgeable, and up-to-date on current events. She had her own convictions on political and economic issues. She had clear and concise values. We chatted for a long time.

She was a delightful revelation. I wondered about it.

I remembered that her husband was a lively and talkative person who dominated every conversation. His dominance was coupled with a loud, booming voice. His wife had chosen to be quiet every time he was around.

The wife was like the sun whose rays were prevented from shining upon people. The cloud, her husband, blocked her warmth.

Are you the sun who cannot shine because of a cloud in your life? Are you the cloud who closes off the glow of your partner, preventing it from nourishing others?

Contemplate who you are.

If you are a cloud, cut down the frequency of your talking. Pause, turn your gaze to your partner, and give her the floor. Learn to encourage your partner's participation. Learn to be a listener, too.

If you are a sun, ask yourself, "Is this person a cloud to me?" Have a little conversation and tell him, "Please don't interrupt me when I'm talking to our friends. Give me time to shine."

When your partner cannot be budged from his 'cloud mode,' develop your own circle of friends. Shine there. Let it be an environment where no clouds are allowed to suppress your thoughts and personality.

People Don't Like Me

Maria and Janice are housekeepers for a wealthy family.

Maria is competent, educated, and knowledgeable. She has been taking charge of things in this household for seven years. On the other hand, Janice is slow and not as efficient as Maria, but she performs her duties with merry countenance.

Maria would not meet the eyes of her employers when they talked to her. She believed that keeping her eyes down was a sign of respect. She also believed that speaking in a low voice was a sign of courtesy. However, her employers had misinterpreted her behavior as a lack of desire to interact. On the other hand, Janice was chatty. She would welcome guests at the door with a big smile and a loud hello. She would also hug them sometimes. She would laugh comfortably when there was humor in the conversation.

This is a comparison of two individuals.

Maria was efficient, yet she felt that people did not like her. She was insecure and anxious about being fired. Her employer misread her as an efficient worker with a bad attitude. Janice was second to Maria in terms of skills and ability, but she carried sunshine throughout the house.

I have been a frequent guest of this family for a long time.

"Observe Janice," I suggested to Maria.

"Why?" she asked.

"Where did you learn to polish furniture? Who taught you how to iron? Who taught you English? Who taught you how to braid?" I asked. She had a name associated with every one of her skills.

"Did you teach Janice these things?"

"Yes, she learned all she knows from me."

"Then learn to smile, greet, laugh, and chat with people from her."

"But that's rude."

"If that were rude, people wouldn't be fond of her. What worked in your homeland doesn't work here. Learn Janice's ways for a higher rate of success."

I must have made sense because Maria stopped complaining. I saw her transform into a cheerful, confident person.

Multibit Screwdriver

While I was growing up, we only had one screwdriver. It was a flathead screwdriver in modern terms. Of course, it worked with flathead screws.

Years passed by. Different types of screws started showing up: Phillips, star-shaped, washer-faced. I had to buy a Phillips screwdriver to deal with Phillips-head screws. There came a time when we had five screwdrivers at home for different types of screws.

Today, I only have one screwdriver. Its handle and stem are the same, but there are little slots in the stem. Different bits snap into it to deal with different types of screws.

In childhood, we developed skills to deal with our parents. If the parents were laid back, the children reciprocated. If the parents were disciplinarian, the children became obedient in carrying out their commands, instructions, and warnings.

Years went by. Our world was filled with teachers, relatives, friends, neighbors, a wife, a husband, parents-in-law, and colleagues. They were a mixture of different personalities who are impossible to deal with uniformly.

We have become like a multibit screwdriver. We make adjustments to the different dispositions of people in our environment. We pick up the specific bit we are going to use in different situations: assertiveness, gentleness, kindness, meekness, and many others, including forgiveness. We learned and grew in our application of these bits. We know that if we do not try, we could end up hurting people and destroying our relationships.

Be like a multibit screwdriver when dealing with different people in varied life situations.

Chapter 13:
Take Time to Ponder

Allow Time for Crystallization

In chemistry, the study of crystals is called crystallography.

The most common crystals are sugar, salt, rock salt, and snowflakes. Other crystals are diamonds and amethysts. You can easily tell what they are by their color and shape.

A crystal is a solid material. When you examine it through a microscope, you can see its molecules arranged in a three-dimensional pattern. It is a form that you can see with your naked eye.

Let's make believe that you're holding two glasses of liquid that look alike. You know that something is in the mixture, but you can't figure out what.

Submerge a wick of cotton into the glass. The wick will slowly absorb the solution. Leave the wick for a few days. You will see crystals of sugar or salt sticking to the wick. Simply put, time helps the syrup to dry up and expose the kinds of crystals in the liquid.

We have a syrup of thoughts and feelings that are hard to figure out. If you take action when everything is muddled in your head, chances are that you will fail to make the right decisions. In the same way, time will help us realize what we're dealing with. What are your options? How can you benefit from what you have? Your desire and motives will be discernable.

In other words, crystallized thoughts and feelings will prevent you from making impulsive decisions that might result in 'syrupy' consequences.

Time to Make Decisions

Chelsea wanted to make a decision regarding her career.

"Asking someone what they want to eat while they're throwing up is not a good idea. Let the stomach settle down first," I told her.

When you're in the middle of a crisis, depression, or any other personal problem, it's not the best time to make decisions for the future.

Why?

Decisions should be made with a cool and collected mind because positive and negative factors must be weighed and considered. A confused, depressed, or troubled mind is not the best source of good judgment.

Postpone making decisions. Let your mind and emotions settle down first.

Rational Reasons for Irrational Acts

Screeeeech!

The car ahead of you came to a dead stop. It gave you no time to hit your brakes. You crashed into the car's rear.

"Damn it! These guys have no driving skills. Stupid son of a b----!" you cursed the driver.

The police came. You learned that the other driver saw a child crossing the street. To avoid hitting the child, he had to slam on his brakes. It was his rational reason for an 'irrational' act, as you had perceived it.

Everybody that we deal with has behaviors that we consider irrational. But when we get the full story, information, and people's point of view, we recognize that their reasons for behaving in such a manner are usually logical.

How would you negotiate your rational reasons for irrational acts? Investigate and mull over the details.

Thought versus Reality

When we have a thought, we often get lost in it.

Actually, our mind is producing words and putting them together to produce ideas. That doesn't make it tangible.

58

Think of a hot dog. Picture it. See the ketchup or the chili on it. You can even smell it.

But the fact is, there is no hot dog before you. Thinking about a hot dog doesn't make it real unless you ransack your refrigerator, take out a hot dog, cook it, and put ketchup or chili on it.

This is true about other things in life. You have to recognize that thoughts are different from reality. Reality can produce thoughts, but thoughts cannot produce reality.

So, when thoughts about people rejecting or disliking you come to mind, ask yourself, "Is this thought reality-based or am I just imagining things?"

If it comes from reality, analyze it and plan what you can do about it. If it's your imagination, kick it out and move on.

Gray Roots

You parted your hair. The roots, which are now grey, became visible to you.

"Hm," you mumbled, "I think they might only be visible to me. Others might not notice."

You're wrong. People are not blind. If you can see it, so can they. Similarly, we are careless about our attitude and behavior. We think that people either don't see it or don't care. This kind of denial is invalid. People *do* see our gray roots as well as our negative attitude and behavior.

Think about a colleague who liked to tell inappropriate jokes at the office. It was more than what you could tolerate, so you walked away. You resolved that, in the future, you would not spend more time with that person. You observed that occasionally, he saw someone roll their eyes. Nevertheless, he kept on with it. He pretended that people were uncomfortable but still enjoying themselves.

Some people don't pick up their share in paying for food or drinks. They always let others spend for them. They make believe that people don't mind. They assume that people are pleased to spend money on them and don't see them as freeloaders.

When a close friend or relative gives you feedback about your behavior or attitude, it is unwise to ignore it. Ponder and ask yourself, "Is it true? Can I do something about it?"

Then take action because someone noticed and pointed it out to you.

Two Kinds of Complaints

Roger was in a meeting for his department. After school hours, he did some shopping in a grocery store.

"I'm sick of my job," he said to the cashier.

While walking to his car, Roger suddenly realized that the cashier had no power to change his job or help him in any way. That meant he was just complaining.

Bringing out a problem, seeking a solution, and applying solutions to the problem is ideal. But complaining is simply airing one's frustrations about a situation without expecting an answer or solution during the moment of expression. Complaining is like exhaling foul emotional air.

Roger asked himself what he was complaining about. He thought about it and figured it out.

Just recently, he had been given a new assignment at work. The project didn't bring him joy. He disliked it. It killed his enthusiasm about going to work.

His acceptance about complaining led him to recognize his disappointment in his recent work. So he went to his boss, communicated his sentiment, and requested a change of assignment. Roger was a very good worker, so the boss readily agreed to his request.

Whenever you find yourself complaining, think about what you need to do and who you need to talk to for solutions. Whining about it just spoils your mood and makes other people see you as a helpless and bitter person.

Chapter 14:
Cautionary Tales

Bookends

Bookends keep a stack of books from falling and help to keep them organized.

Uncontrolled spending destroys the family budget. Difficulties follow. Borrowing is inevitable. Peace of mind flies out the window. The person's social standing among friends and relatives is tainted.

A determined decision to set up and observe reasonable boundaries for your family's financial habits is like putting up bookends. This balance will keep your family from over and underspending.

Extremes are disruptive to family harmony, so be cautious. It pays to walk the middle path the way books stand upright between two bookends.

Can I Prevent Interference in My Life?

"My family gives me advice. If I don't follow it, I feel bad. What should I do?"

You had solicited their help in the past. They gave you suggestions according to their value system and their own approach to life. Those worked for you then.

However, now that you are an adult, your knowledge base and value system have changed; hence, you are feeling different.

You're still disclosing things to them, so they give you advice because they care. The problem is that you consider their words to be orders and have begun resenting it.

In reality, they are not orders. You only perceived them as such because of your old mindset that you are a child who must follow what they say.

If you think that your friends and family can help, go ahead and open up. But words of caution: be discreet so you don't invite intrusion. Ponder this thought from W.E. Norris:

"If your lips would keep from slips,
Five things observe with care;
To whom you speak, of whom you speak
And how, and when, and where."

Warn Others

Exhaustion, loads of work, headaches, PMS. These things may put a person in a bad mood from time to time.

These are not disabling. The person is still able to function, though she may be wearing furrowed brows. Her eyes are downcast. She doesn't make eye contact, nor does she smile. She is unaware of her facial expressions and general demeanor.

Her bad mood has nothing to do with her surroundings. Nevertheless, people around her tend to personalize her unusual tight-lipped disposition.

The following day, the person's headache is gone and she's back to her normal self. However, the people around her are quiet and tense. She doesn't understand why everybody seems so distant.

This is the start of a new negative cycle.

When you are feeling physically unwell, it is safe to tell people the following:

"Please don't mind my bad mood today. I'm nauseated."

"Don't mind me today. I am so tired."

A woman could say, "Disregard my mood today. It's PMS."

Help prevent one bad mood from pervading your home or office environment. Forewarn people. It doesn't make sense to keep them wondering if they did something to upset you.

Watch for Signs

I was walking down a hospital corridor and saw a woman coming toward me. She looked to her left and saw a signboard. She stopped to read it for a couple of seconds, and then she turned back. The signboard made her aware that she was going in the wrong direction. She quickly retraced her steps and saved time.

When we travel on the highway, we watch for various signs. The minute we miss our exit, we change direction. When we hear the whistle of a tea kettle, we turn off the stove. When the thermometer registers a fever, we take medicine.

Signs point us in the right direction when we respect their guidance.

What do signs tell you about your relationships? Are you heading in the wrong direction? What are you planning to do about it?

If you are unhappy, tense, irritated, or pressured, be alert! These are signs that are saying, "You are not on the right track. Something is wrong!"

Take immediate action to reverse your course. If you have been working hard and don't know how to take a breather, the signboard says, 'Play a While.' If you have been gambling and drinking too much alcohol, the signboard says, 'Slow Down.' If you easily fall into harsh arguments with those around you, the signboard says, 'Rectify It.'

Watch your signs. They point to good pathways.

Chapter 15:
Reframing Your Mindset

Misguided Expectations

Many frustrations in life come from fallacies.

One example: "Everybody's behavior should be judged by comparing it with mine. I am the standard by which everything must be measured. If anybody is not like me, there's something wrong with them."

When people are different from us, we tend not to like them. If they are slow, they irritate us. If they are fast, they irritate us. If they are loud, we complain. If they are silent, we complain. If they eat a lot, we look down on them and say, "He is a glutton." If they are picky eaters, we look down on them and say, "She's anorexic." If they spend more on clothes than we do, we say, "How wasteful!" If they dress simply, we say, "Ugh, you should see the way they dress. What do they do with their money?" If they have different morals, we frown and say, "How rigid!" If they are relaxed, we frown and say, "How irresponsible."

A meeting of four couples for dinner may center on someone else's choices that are a shade different from their own. "I hate that mauve wallpaper. It gets on my nerves," they say.

Among billions of people, there are no set standards. Don't fall into the trap of thinking you're the standard. Embrace that everyone is different and unique.

Travelers

We are all travelers. I was born in the forties; now I am in the 21st century. We travel from one stage of life to another: infancy, adolescence, adulthood, middle age, and old age.

We travel from place to place. I was born in Pakistan; I moved to India, then to America. We travel in relationships. I was close to my aunts, uncles, and cousins. Many of them passed away while others moved far away. Other people have come to fill the void they left in my life. We travel in education: elementary to high school, college, graduate studies, and on to continuing education.

We travel in maturity. I made mistakes in judgment here and there. As the years passed, I have grown from uncertainty to stability, from unsteady to consistent. We travel in our health. I was a healthy young man who preferred to run rather than walk. Now I am an older man and it hurts when I run. We travel in time, from the past, to the present, to the future, and to our final destination: death.

Do you see? Life is a constant journey in different aspects and on many levels. So, when you lose a job, say, "I have left one location. It's time to go to the next destination." When you have broken relationships, say, "It's about time to move forward to another relationship." When you have a setback in your health, say, "I'm traveling from one state of health to another."

Different Perspectives

Alexander the Great, Jesus, and Buddha saw the moon when they walked on earth. The moon was worshipped as the 'moon god' in those days.

Years later, we found out that the moon is made of stone. Its worshipers have changed their understanding and perception. Their awe and devotion turned into matter-of-fact knowledge about a heavenly body.

When we were children, we put our parents on a pedestal. We saw them as perfect people. We regarded them with awe and considered them 'the best.'

If one of our classmates said that babies were made through sex and our parents had us that way, we fumed and said, "My parents aren't like that."

Years went by. We grew and recognized that the information about sex from our older friends was correct. One by one, we saw our parents' imperfections. They were not the best at everything as we had believed in childhood.

There's nothing wrong with changed perception. Don't feel guilty. The improved understanding of former moon worshippers did not make the moon crash to earth. It's still in the sky—forever. In like manner, the discovery of our parents' imperfections did not make us respect them less. They are in our hearts—forever.

Flowers on the Grave

Chrysanthemums. Tulips. Roses. Orchids.

No matter how lovely these flowers are, a dead person doesn't appreciate them. The dead body is beyond caring. However, when you go to a graveyard, you see different types of flowers decorating many graves.

The living visit and put flowers there as an expression of their love and affection for departed loved ones. The gesture brings them comfort.

Are your relationships with other living beings 'dead' due to resentment, neglect, or disregard?

Decorate the 'graves' of your relationships with friends and family with renewed contact. They still have the ability to notice your efforts and smell the flowers.

Visit the graves of the dead as well as the graves of dead relationships.

Why Suicide? He Had Everything

A person killed himself.

People wondered, "He had fame, money, children, a wife, cars, a great house, and good social standing. Why did he do it?"

When something is very close to our eyes, it blocks our vision. Your palms are small, but if you cover your eyes with them, you can't see.

When a person is despondent, it's like his eyes are covered by his palms. His palms hide the world from him. He cannot see his loved ones, the sky, the trees, or the flowers. A few minutes before suicide, everything that the person possesses would cease to be of value to him. He is focused on what he cannot solve.

If he opens up, talks, or lets time pass, he can restore his self-created blindness to seeing the joys of life.

A Hole in the Bucket

There was a sturdy water container called Bucket. His master made much use of him.

Bucket developed a hole in his bottom. His master discarded him beside a flowerpot.

Bucket thought about this hole day in and day out. He became depressed and hopeless.

"Hey, Bucket, I'm Flowerpot," the pot introduced himself.

Bucket did not acknowledge Flowerpot.

"Why are you so quiet, Bucket?" Pot persisted.

At last, Bucket opened his mouth to tell his sad story.

"I am useless since I developed a hole in my bottom. I want to die," he said and started crying.

"I don't understand. You said you were useless. I'm here to tell you that you're not!" Pot said in a calm voice.

"I can no longer hold any liquid. What do you call that?" Bucket answered.

"True, you cannot carry water. I, too, have a hole in my bottom. However, look what I'm doing today. I am beautifying the master's garden! Can you see how many flowers I hold?" the flowerpot added.

"What do you mean?" Bucket asked, wiping away his tears.

"I was also a bucket before I became a flowerpot. I could no longer carry water when I got this hole. Seeing my other potential, the master had me hold his plants instead," Pot answered.

"Maybe the master took you out from storage so he can use you for his ornamental plant," Pot encouraged.

People lose sight of the functioning parts of their body when they lose the use of a body part.

Have you lost one of your legs? You still have both hands, both eyes, both ears, and a sound mind.

Have you lost a hand? You still have both legs—and you are not blind, you are not deaf, you are not mute, and you have a sound mind. Do not let the good, functioning parts rot in stagnation. Move on. Life is waiting for you to join in again.

The Walnut Tree and the Bamboo

The trunk of a walnut tree and a bamboo differ from each other. The walnut is huge, but it can break in bad weather because of its rigidity. The bamboo is slim, but it is hardly uprooted by fierce winds because it bends low and sways when the wind blows.

Human beings are like walnut and bamboo trees in terms of body types. Some are inherently big-boned. They subject their bodies to exercise and diet, but nothing can be done about their large body structures. Some people have naturally slim body structures. Though they may eat like a horse, they still look like a giraffe's neck.

Big-breasted and wide-hipped Caucasian women are admired in Asia where women want to have a larger physique. Asian women are admired in Caucasian countries where bodies slim as a twig are highly desired and considered attractive. A slender, small-boned Asian woman who goes to a Caucasian community would be envied. A Caucasian woman would look like a goddess in the eyes of many Asians.

If you are insecure with your build, shouldn't you have a more important consideration? How about a body that is healthy and full of energy? How about a pleasant disposition that reflects inner peace? How about being effective at what you do? These are much more important matters to dwell on.

The walnut is majestic and the bamboo is flexible. Be content, whether you are like a bamboo or a walnut tree. Treasure your own uniqueness.

Don't Take it So Seriously

Have you noticed that, over a period of time, clothes, bags, pieces of jewelry, and even women's makeup have changed?

Fashion comes and goes, and it comes back again. It's here today, it's passé tomorrow. However, before you can take a fashionable breath, it rushes back again.

When you see your costly wardrobe, say to yourself, "This style will come back within my lifetime." It won't make you feel so bad to keep it for use in the future.

Understanding the cycle of fashion will help you tolerate your current wardrobe with more patience. Understanding can remove insecurity and inferiority from your mind.

Make the best of fashion. There's no reason to be frustrated when it changes. It usually comes around again.

Learning French Cuisine

Robin joined a psychiatric residency training program in New York. Things were going well until two supervisors joined to oversee his cases.

Robin was treating a seven-year-old girl with a doll phobia at the time.

One supervisor, a behaviorist, dealt with behavior. He suggested that the patient who is afraid of dolls should be progressively exposed to the doll—50, 40, 30, 20, and 10 yards away from it. Robin has to reward an M&M every time the little girl steps closer to the doll. The other supervisor, a psychoanalyst, dealt with *why* the patient has doll phobia.

From the psychoanalyst: "The behaviorist's suggestion is superficial. It doesn't address the cause."

From the behaviorist: "How long will it take for psychoanalytical technique to scrutinize the details of the cause?

Knowing the cause is unnecessary. The goal is for the child to eventually touch, embrace, and play with dolls. Extinguishing her fear is most important."

Robin wanted to learn, but he was confused with the conflicting methods. He felt that there must be a combination of good from both sides.

"Your goal is correct. But you're in training and in the learning phase right now. That being so, you have to learn all techniques in their purest form," I said.

"Let's make believe that a student is obtaining a Master's Degree in Culinary Science. In one rotation, he went to a French chef who refused to use ingredients used in fast foods. Should the student have to learn pure French cooking, knowing that he will be opening a fast food business later?" I asked.

"In the next rotation, he learned fast food cooking. Still later, he learned ethnic cuisines. He must be aware of *every* style. He could use any one of them or come up with a fusion of foods in his own style," I added.

The explanation made sense to Robin. He went back to his psychiatric 'cooking classes' with a clear head. He was no longer confused and angry every time he heard the inflexible 'master chefs,' who were each teaching him their pure cuisine.

Life is Predictable

Death due to an accident is a reminder of our mortality. In this down moment, we become anxious and depressed. In times like these, we tend to label life as 'unpredictable.' We remember the tragedies that happened, then fear and insecurity prevail.

Do a small experiment.

Stand up on a bridge that crosses a major highway like Garden State Parkway. You can see the eight-lane highway from up there. When you have the endurance to stay there for an hour, you can see the predictability of cars on that highway: thousands pass by without an accident.

Bring your mind to the fact that you have been on the road two hours a day for 365 days a year. Multiply it by 20 years of your life. Except those days that you had an accident, your life was predictable: you and your car remained intact.

There is a rise in the population of countries where contraceptives are not allowed. There are more births than deaths. Predictable results. Countries where contraception is used have a controlled population. People are healthier; life span is longer. Predictable results.

Look at life with a bird's eye view to see the general state of things.

Your life has not always been dark, right? Your sunny days outnumber your cloudy days.

Climb the Tree, Don't Touch the Sky

Job loss and broken relationships often demoralize a person.

I was talking to Shania, encouraging her to pursue further education and do things that were within her reach. It involved money and time, which she had aplenty, and patience and hard work, which were her attributes.

Shania sobbed with desperation, "I can't. It's impossible."

I made it easy for her to understand. I said, "What I'm asking you is only to go up a tree, not touch the sky."

She decided to go to college.

Vacation without Vacation

Do you remember when you planned your last vacation? Excitement was apparent in the whole family. A vibrant atmosphere enveloped every discussion about the place, transportation, hotel accommodations, and the spots to visit. Every family member's face was well-lit by a ready smile when bits and pieces of the plan sprang up during regular conversations.

While doing your routine work, your mind was seeing a white beach. How you wanted to feel the sand on your feet. Your skin tingled at the combination of clear seawater and sunshine.

These thoughts infused strength that energized your body. It made your every step light as a feather. You had not even bought tickets or booked your hotel, but just anticipating your experience did something good for your spirit.

The calm, refreshing scene gives gladness to your heart. Scientifically, this is called relaxation by visualization.

Off and on, bring that calm scene to your mind. It's just like taking a vacation in your own home.

Humility Seeds

When I went for a walk one day, I saw seedless sunflowers of about four inches in diameter. They were standing tall, facing the sun.

I returned from my walk and the sun had moved across the sky. The sunflowers were still standing tall and straight, facing the sun. They had followed the sun across the sky. That's why we call them sunflowers.

As weeks passed by, I watched them grow bigger. They were nine inches in diameter. Their flowers were not facing the sun anymore, but facing the ground.

Why?

They were heavily laden with seeds.

Young and inexperienced people are full of pride, though they have nothing much to their name and nothing much to offer the world. With age and experience, people gain wisdom, knowledge, and develop the virtue of humility. They recognize their limits. The seeds of achievement and maturity bow our heads in humility.

Change 'Either/Or' to 'And'

"Was my father a good father or a bad one?"

Rob had been bugged with this thought all his life. His father was a very rigid disciplinarian at home, but he was a well-respected authority in his field.

When his father died, Rob had inner conflict about following in the same path. This difficulty stemmed from his resentment toward his father, who made him feel insignificant. He was not sure how to 'label' him. Was he a good or a bad father?

I said, "Rob, don't think in terms of your dad being good *or* bad. Accept his good traits as well as his flaws. Get out of the either/or conflict. Accept reality by using the word 'and.' That means replace the 'either/or' in your reasoning with 'and.' It goes like this: 'He was a distinguished doctor *and* a strict father.'"

Rob reported that the 'and' has helped him move on. His resentment decreased. Every time the conflict would pester him, he would immediately shift to, "My father was a good doctor to his patients and a bad father to his son. He was an accomplished doctor and a rotten father to me."

From a Different Planet

"The situation is life-threatening, but they just don't care," Jean complained.

If there is one thing that Jean feels strongly about, it's safety. She is highly alert to possible danger and quick to point it out. But people just laugh off her warnings.

Why is Jean so passionate about safety?

She had witnessed an accident. She saw a co-worker crushed by a machine, which made her very safety conscious. People's nonchalance irritated and frustrated her.

It's like Jean is from a different planet. People have not experienced life on that planet, so they can't relate. When Jean recognizes this truth, she may not be bothered so much.

The same applies to people who came through depression, former alcoholics, former drug addicts, or a person who is dying due to cigarette smoking. They may tend to be 'preachy' because of their experience, but the recipient may feel criticized by the constant reminder.

"I understand your passion about it. I understand where you're coming from," says the recipient.

74

"I understand your lukewarm attitude. You can't fully comprehend because you haven't tasted the reality of it," says the talker.

The Penthouse

My office is located on the second floor of a four-story building.

I was waiting for the elevator one day. A woman wearing a flowery jacket was also in the lobby. She was probably a nurse or office staff.

She entered the lift first.

"What floor?" she asked me after she pressed the button for the 4th floor.

"Two, please," I said and added, "Are you going to the top?"

"Yes, to the penthouse."

"Which office is it?"

"Dr. Abraham's."

"I know him. He's a great doctor."

"Yes, he is. I've worked for him for 19 years now."

I was still thinking about the woman as I walked toward my office.

Why?

Her attitude fascinated me. We had no 'penthouse' in the building. Her saying so showed her attitude toward her work. She was vibrant and lively. Overall, she had a light disposition.

Of course, who wouldn't be happy when they're on their way to a nice, elegant, posh penthouse? What a positive attitude!

Your Ability to Adjust

Whatttt? OMG! Gray hair?!

You remember your strong reaction the very first time you saw gray hair on your head. You could hardly believe it. You went around the house in shock, showing the gray hair to anyone who was around.

Time passed. The number of gray strands outnumbered the others. Do you remember your reaction?

You ceased to care. You learned to tolerate changes in your body, face, and on your head.

It was the same with baldness. It was hard for you to accept the reality at first, but then you got used to it. Though you can no longer play tennis the way you used to, you were able to slowly adapt to that reality as well.

Anything new that you don't like is bothersome, but your ability to tolerate it is exceptional.

Shock and grief?

No worries. Remember, they will come and go... and you know that you will get used to it soon.

Natural

Roger is oversold on the philosophy of living natural. He eats only raw vegetables and sushi with raw fish. He drinks only unpasteurized milk.

Uncooked food gave him a noisy, painful stomach. He would have diarrhea. However, he called it 'cleansing.'

"The uncooked food is causing your stomach problems. The human intestine cannot digest so much uncooked food," I explained.

But he kept propounding the 'natural' philosophy.

"If you want to be really natural, don't use soap, shampoo, deodorant, toothpaste, toothbrush, and toilet paper. Stay natural and smell natural," I urged.

He had to rethink his philosophy; otherwise, it would backfire when he goes beyond the rational limits.

Chapter 16:
I Love Me, I Love Me Not

Hello Me, Nice to Meet You

You have learned how to get along with clients, bosses, employees, family members, and friends, but no one has taught you how to manage the person who repeatedly criticizes you. Instead of encouraging you and boosting your confidence, he sows doubts in you.

Who is he? He is YOU.

You live with yourself 24/7. You say, "I know myself well." In the same breath, you say, "I don't know if I can do it." This is a strange combination, isn't it?

Here is an example of your self-contradiction.

You have always done your best at your job because you wanted your company to consider you for a promotion. However, when you were assigned important work, you saw it as an attempt by management to make you fail. You have always worked hard so that your boss would notice you, but every time he calls you to his office, you are prepared to get fired. Isn't that weird?

See difficulties on the job as opportunities to prove that you are good and capable. Rise to the occasion!

Every morning, look in the mirror and meet yourself. Say, "Hello me, nice to meet you! Let's make the best of this great day!"

Hanging in There

I often meet my friends, acquaintances, and colleagues in the hospital parking lot and corridors.

"How are you doing?" I ask.

"Hanging in there," is the usual answer.

"Hanging in there," always transports my mind to a cat stuck on a precipice, ready to fall into a big crevice and die.

"Hanging in there," means barely making it. Barely making it means ready to fall. Ready to fall is ready to self-destruct and die. It's a negative message.

I know from personal experience that those people are far from 'just barely making it.' They are active, successful professionals and responsible individuals.

Next time when someone asks how you're doing, what will you say?

Surprise them by saying, "Succeeding," "Having a wonderful day," "Life is beautiful!" or, "God is kind;" anything that ignites positive vibration.

Don't curse yourself by saying, "Hanging in there."

Understand Your Partner

You're living with a partner. Your partner makes you unhappy at times because he often criticizes you and puts you down. If you want to have fun, he reminds you of undone work. When you work, he tells you that you're slow. If you go fast, he says you're not good enough. If you initiate a conversation with someone, he whispers, "Stop! People don't like you."

Would you stand up to this person, please? Sit down with him and say, "We need to have a serious talk."

Open up about your anger at his constant put-downs and efforts to isolate you from others.

Yell at him if you have to!

Guess who that partner is?

Who else? It's YOU.

In the movies, we've all seen an angel on one shoulder and a devil on the other. They talk to the person. That's what I'm talking about. The angel, the positive, is 'you.' The devil, the negative, is also 'you.'

Your positive self encourages you to go out, meet people, refresh and expand yourself. He guides you to make a list of feasible tasks. When you finish your tasks, he makes you feel satisfied with what you have accomplished. He doesn't bother you with complaints about your past or frighten you about tomorrow.

Work with your positive self. Write down the criticisms of the negative side and see how real they are. Let the positive partner deal with the negative partner to create balance and make things right.

Stop Degrading Yourself

"I'm a blabbermouth," Yolanda said.

Sometimes, we crack jokes and make fun of ourselves to make people laugh. We call it a 'sense of humor.' Oftentimes, the motive is to impress others and make them like us. However, the habit of saying bad things about ourselves can backfire.

Words have their own power if repeated. Our ugly words for ourselves will register with people. Our descriptions will take shape in their minds every time they look at us or think about us.

During a get-together, someone loudly said to Yolanda, "Shut up, blabbermouth! What do you know?" That hurt her.

When you disrespect yourself, don't be surprised if others disrespect you, too. Why shouldn't they when you so easily do it to yourself? Therefore, avoid derogatory remarks toward yourself.

Don't splash mud on your freshly polished shoes just to make others laugh. Walk with shiny shoes.

Feeling Inferior

Marina has a habit of putting herself down and keeping herself last. She tolerates put-downs from others without protest. She thinks she deserves it because she thinks she's inferior.

Water evaporates and forms rain clouds. Rain pours. If a raindrop is part of the same body of water, it's the same as the other drops. You are the same with the rest of humanity. You have the same origin we all have.

Some raindrops fall on rice paddies, on the rooftops of palaces, on cemented highways, and many other places. When raindrops fall in a mud puddle or on a rose petal, they look different but have the same element: water. Did you know that a chemist could distill 100% pure water out of mud?

It doesn't matter what a person's situation is. He can rise or stay down based on his mindset. If you believe that there are deficiencies in you, recognize them and work to rise above them with the help of training, education, and therapy.

Stop your 'nothing can be done about it' thoughts. Rise from your abused situation. Inferiority exists only in your mind. In reality, nobody can trample on you... unless you allow them to.

Chapter 17:
Keep Your Tempter; I Don't Want It

Porcupines are Like Scared Rabbits

A long time ago, fluffy rabbits existed. Predators attacked them. The rabbits thought that developing needles would protect them; hence came porcupines. (Kidding!)

People love to have rabbits as pets. They are silky and don't complain when being cuddled. People also write lovely stories about rabbits and almost worship them on Easter. Rabbits even have their own men's magazine. (Kidding again!)

On the other hand, nobody cares to be near porcupines. Porcupines also don't usually get close to humans for affection.

Some people are like rabbits. They don't know how to assert themselves, including saying no to things they dislike. If you push, they will express it through aggression. If you talk to them, they yell at you. If you look at them, they stare back with furrowed brows. They do this to cover, protect, and preserve their soft, gentle nature.

In doing so, they are like a rabbit that suddenly turned into a porcupine. They push everybody away from them. They become lonely and isolated because nobody wants to get close.

Rabbits and porcupines can't change their appearance, but humans have the ability to change. We can be people who are soft, yet assertive. We can state our convictions without fear. We can express our ideas in a non-abrasive manner, using appropriate words and a gentle voice.

People are oftentimes insensitive. They are unaware that what they ask is uncomfortable. When you suddenly grow spikes of anger, hostility, yelling, cursing, or withdrawing from them, they feel hurt because they don't understand.

"I asked to borrow her necklace for the evening, but she chewed me out," a loved one or a friend may say.

If somebody manipulates and wants to extract things from you including money, take control. Stand your ground without shedding your cuddly rabbit fur for porcupine needles. Take your stand gently but firmly. You don't have to say it in so many words or explain lengthily. "No, I don't want to," will do; and that's it.

Taut Guitar Strings

If you tighten the strings of a guitar to the point that they become too taut, the guitar will make a humming sound when there are slight movements in the air. Even the whirr of an electric fan can make them hum. If you tighten them some more, they snap.

When a person is hungry, angry, rushed, broke, or has premenstrual tension, she is like the taut string of a guitar. She becomes short-tempered and sensitive to people's words and behavior. She's like a newly awakened dragon. Steam comes out of her nostrils. She's ready to jump down people's throats, even without a valid cause. Her mental sewage unfairly flows on them.

When you feel that your senses are stretched to their limit, walk away, take a pause, think, and focus.

What am I doing? What am I saying? What caused this?

Mental havoc never helps. It doesn't allow space for rational thoughts.

So, loosen your tight wires. Divert. Drink a glass of water. Go to the bathroom. Eat a candy bar. Sit down calmly and discuss what's bothering you.

Remember, we can always control how we express our agitation. So, relax; otherwise your wires will hum even when a bug flies by.

Watch for the Tornado

Tornadoes are deadly. Authorities warn people about an incoming tornado. They advise people to stay in their basements for safety. People unplug all their appliances to prevent fire or damage.

Individual people experience tornadoes of depression, anger, self-pity, or anxiety, to name a few.

When blood rushes to your head and you're ready to bite someone's head off, it's a warning of anger. Before it erupts, go to the 'basement.' This could be any quiet place where you get a drink of water, eat, or do something to calm your nerves. You can minimize damage by unplugging from people who might be casualties.

Once your emotional tornado has subsided, reevaluate the situation and take action with a sound mind.

Anger as a Handgun

Police officers are trained to use their guns in appropriate situations. Some people who are licensed to carry guns don't have such extensive training and discipline.

When you are angry, it's like carrying a fully loaded gun. The most important thing to ask is, "Am I a trained policeman or am I among other people?"

Maybe you came home and your spouse did something that irritated you. You unloaded your anger bullets into her.

Uncontrolled firing could injure the target badly and kill the relationship. It was irresponsible gun handling.

Next time you're fuming, fire and empty it out into the air. How do you do that?

Go to a quiet place. Write down your anger on a sheet of paper or dictate it onto a voice recorder. Your anger will lose its force. It's like taking the bullets out of the gun. Though the blame and complaints remain in your head, the anger attached to them dissipates.

When you practice this every time your emotions want to run amok, you're like a trained police officer, disciplined in handling an anger gun.

Controlling Your Expression of Negative Emotions

Anger, sadness, and anxiety are part of the daily struggle, but yelling, screaming, crying, and verbal tirades have negative consequences.

A couple in the middle of an argument heard the doorbell ring. They glanced at each other and were quiet for a few seconds. They collected themselves and received the visitor. They went back to where they left off when the visitor was gone.

A woman was sitting in church, listening to a sermon. She glanced out the window. Her child was on her way toward the gate. She stifled her gasp and got up. Once she was outside, she ran like a cheetah and collected her child.

When you are going for an interview, you can choose to leave your bad mood at home to impress the interviewer.

Do you see what I'm getting at? Some things can be controlled for social propriety. However, selectivity disappears when a person is distressed. Chronic depression reduces emotional restraints. A nurse who arrived late or a misplaced watch can bring out episodes of crying.

When a person feels better, he might still think that those emotional expressions are appropriate and necessary. The fact is, this is not so.

Antiperspirant of Emotions

The following was an exchange between two men in a TV deodorant ad in the past.

"I don't use antiperspirant," one man said.

"Yes, I know!" the other man said.

Perspiration is a natural process in the human body. The underarm is a part that sweats a lot. Its smell is a killer! People who are aware of this always make sure they use antiperspirant. It subdues the brute power of their scent.

On the other hand, people who are insensitive don't care to use any. They 'punish' others with their sadistic smell.

Ben and Bob are friends who had some different opinions about their common business. Both of them had gone on vacation with their respective families.

One wife said, "It was a remarkable, fun vacation!"

How come?

Ben and Bob said to each other, "Let's decide not to discuss business on vacation for the sake of our families."

They knew that even just a word about their differences would spark a debate that would surely spoil the vacation. So they shook hands on this agreement. The fun vacation was made possible.

Though their minds were full of emotional sweat, both hindered its flow through the deodorant of control.

We live in a complex world that is full of imperfect relationships. Disagreements are inevitable.

Chapter 18:
Tact and Consideration

Free Air for the Ego

Free air is a selling strategy. Free air pumping entices you to go to a gas station. While you're there, you buy gas from them. The gas station takes money from you. It has benefited from its free air service.

Praising a person is like filling him with air. If you inflate his ego a bit with genuine praise or appreciation, he will feel good about himself and about you. It fosters goodwill. It increases cooperation from people.

Power Strips and Relationships

My wife plugged her iPad, phone, video game, and her back-up alarm system into a power strip that she uses. There were four wires coming from the power strip into these four electronic devices. When she removed the gadgets the next day, they were dead. She discovered that the power strip had not been connected to an outlet.

There are metaphorical 'power strips' that give power to relationships. These can be sponsoring or attending a business dinner or networking with businessmen on various ventures. However, the electrical juice of goodwill does not flow from here.

What is the electrical juice of goodwill? These are deeds you do for a person because you love him. Giving him a gift on special occasions, inviting him for a family dinner, attending the funeral of his mother or father, and taking some food to his home when he is sick when you know that nobody is there to cook for him are some examples. It also includes visiting him when his health is in trouble, when he is financially burdened, or when he has lost his job. These things are like power strips connected to electrical power, supplying energy to the relationship.

Couple your business efforts with humane acts; otherwise, the relationship will not flourish.

Italian Beret

I am semi-bald, but my head looks okay to me. Freshly washed hair, a comb, and a mild hair spray make me feel good.

On the weekends, I let loose by walking around the house in my pajamas with my disheveled hair looking like dried-up ramen noodles.

When my wife asks me to get a gallon of milk from the supermarket, I simply put on an Italian beret – a gift from my kids – to cover the 'noodles.' In the supermarket, I frequently receive appreciative glances for my beret, or even a comment like, "That looks beautiful."

Beautiful? Yes, my beret is. It covers the noodles hiding underneath!

When I return home, I remove the beret and walk around again with my exposed, dried up ramen-noodle-Mohawk.

How does putting on a beret work in terms of human attitude?

We are in a good mood most of the time. We are pleasant with a ready smile. People around us relate to us well. But we have our bad days once in a while. A lot of stuff fills our mind and we feel like snapping at people for no reason.

When we recognize our bad mood and its effect on others, we can use a beret to cover it. The beret is a smile, a warm hello, or an eager handshake, and it can keep others from seeing our Mohawk of nasty feelings. Our smile brings a positive response and prevents alienation from others.

When you are in a nasty mood, recognize it and put on your smile beret.

Q-Tips

Leo Gerstenzang, a Polish-born American, invented three-inch long, double-tipped plastic cotton swabs in 1923. This item is now used internationally. A small amount of cotton is wrapped around the ends of a three-inch long stick. Being covered with a soft material, it becomes useful for applying eye makeup and for medicinal solutions. It is also used in baby care.

A small, thin, hard stick that goes into the ear can damage the ear's internal canal. It may also scratch the skin of the face or the surface of the eye. However, the gentle, protective cotton around the tip makes it safer.

The Q-tip has a combination of sturdiness and softness. The stick is hard, but the cotton-wrapped ends give a gentle touch on the surface.

A person can be like a Q-tip. He can have strong principles, beliefs, or morals. The ability to communicate these persuasions in a non-abrasive or non-offensive manner is a remarkable skill.

Become like a Q-tip. Have a firm foundation internally but a gentle manner externally.

Why is the Dog So Quiet?

Toofy, our dog, barks when somebody walks in the door. Then he sits down quietly the moment the visitor is settled.

However, every time my son Gautam visits us, Toofy goes crazy. He barks, jumps, and runs around the house to welcome him. Gautam is equally excited and calls Toofy's name over and over. He hugs, kisses, talks, taps, and cuddles Toofy. He runs to the lawn, inviting Toofy to fetch the ball.

Toofy's behavior is different when he is with Gautam. He is reciprocating Gautam's playful behavior.

Why am I talking about our dog?

There have probably been times when you visited friends and felt unwelcomed. You sensed that their reception lacked warmth. Your friend just sat on his sofa like a bump on a log. Then you wondered, "Why the shabby treatment?"

Look at your own behavior toward the friend you visited. Was it like our guests toward Toofy? Were you a quiet, boring person who had nothing to say? When you opened your mouth, all the listener heard was misery, disease, bad weather, and your problems. Maybe you were also bad-mouthing your friends.

Are you a person who shares jokes, laughter, and good news about the world? Do you focus on good news about your friends, neighborhood, town, an art exhibit, or a new radio show?

If you are like Gautam, you will bring cheer to the dog and the dog will show happy responses. If you are like the other guests who walked in, sat down, and expected the dog to be friendly, it's not going to happen.

Do you make people chuckle, smirk, smile, cry, or yawn? What do you bring to your friends' tables?

Designing Signage in Your Life

A hospital hired an installer to replace old signs.

"It will take one year to complete the installation," the installer said.

The chief of the hospital was surprised. He expected the job to be completed in a month.

The installer explained, "I'm not going to duplicate your current signs. I'm going to make the hospital a visitor-friendly place."

He inquired at doctors' offices, the laboratory, and x-ray departments about how frequently their patients were late for appointments.

He wore a, "May I help you?" sign and stood in different places in the hospital. People would ask him for directions to different departments.

He stood near the old signs and observed people's facial expressions. When he found people squinting their eyes and scratching their heads, he would ask, "What's the problem?" He would hear complaints like, "The Information Desk told me that the x-ray department is on the first floor. I can't find it anywhere."

He stood near the elevator. It carried a list of nine destinations in alphabetical order: A for admission, B for basement, C for cardiology, D for dining hall, F for foyer, and so on. He timed people to see how many seconds it took them to figure out which button to press.

He noticed that 70% of the people pressed 'cafeteria,' 20% pressed 'foyer,' and 5% pressed 'cardiology.' So instead of doing them alphabetically, he put 'cafeteria' first, 'foyer' second, and 'cardiology' third. As soon as the new signage was put up, he noticed that people were quick to press buttons.

He designed the signage according to people's needs. Having listened to their confusion and difficulties, he was able to reduce the frequency of their lateness to appointments. He saved the hospital thousands of dollars in wasted time.

In human relationships, do you ask your spouse, family members, or customers how you can help them?

You gave gifts to children on Christmas. Did you find out whether they have used them?

Have you asked for feedback from your family about how they would like dinner to be modified next time?

Have you asked your mate's preference when you buy clothes for her?

Have you asked your mate how he likes to be kissed?

Opening yourself to feedback about how your behavior is affecting others is a step toward improved relationships.

Be the signage specialist of human relations.

Gas

A person expelled gas and people scampered out of the room. Hankies found their way to noses. People held their breath until they were blue in the face.

There are gases that do not have a strong smell, like propane, but they are deadly because they're highly flammable.

In life, there are two kinds of people.

There are the toxic kind, loud toxic and silent toxic. The loud type creates a stink by talking indiscriminately. Others are quiet; you don't hear anything from them, but you can see that they are seething with resentment by their facial expressions and body language. You don't feel good being with them.

Then there are the fragrant kind. Their presence creates a pleasant atmosphere. People want to keep them around because they disperse coolness into the air by their pleasant demeanor and gracious words.

Are you like a fart or a flower?

Now Here, Now Gone

People relate differently.

Meeting friends brings joy. Later, they keep in touch with phone calls and emails. They send greetings on birthdays and wedding anniversaries. They relate infrequently but consistently.

To others, meeting with friends means relating intensely. They make others feel like VIPs. They are generous with gifts and praise. But as soon as they are not present face to face, you do not hear from them. If you initiate contact through phone calls, text messages, or emails, they respond in an obligatory manner that makes you wonder, "Is this the same person I was with just a week ago?" Their reception makes you question whether the good times they shared with you were fake.

How about you? Are you a person who keeps in moderate but consistent contact with your friends? Are you one who gives so much that it exhausts you?

You are a busy person and cannot interact at an intense level for an extended period. You don't initiate or receive phone calls because you don't want to get stuck for an hour. The longer you stay in silent mode, the more you hesitate to interact again. It's uncomfortable to reply to questions like, "Where were you all this time?"

You can control this awkward cycle. Don't do and give more than you can. Give only realistically and consistently.

Understand that you're inclined to go to both extremes: extreme giving and extreme withdrawal. It will help you recognize your vulnerability and lead you to modify your behavior.

Look at Me, Please

Someone is talking to you, but you're looking at the floor.

Would he think that you're interested?

Nope.

Being engrossed in your shoelaces will make a person feel that he is unimportant to you.

If you have experienced this from the other perspective, you know what I'm talking about. Rejection is never a good feeling, is it?

Even if you were actually listening and every spoken word did register, the other person would walk away with the wrong impression because you were looking down.

Don't diminish a person's sense of self-value. When he's talking to you, hold off looking at your cellphone or anything but him. Someone who gives his time to speak with you deserves to be given attention. Look him in the eye as he's speaking to you.

Emotional Wardrobe

Most people own plenty of clothes, but only a few can be considered well-dressed.

Well-dressed people properly match clothes, and they are careful to wear the right clothing for the right occasion.

Being well-dressed does not necessarily mean new and expensive clothes. It simply means coordinating the right colors and not being over-dressed or under-dressed for the occasion.

Let's translate this to human relationships.

Some of us have forgotten some simple courtesies like saying, "Good morning," "Thank you," and other polite things. Some of us make no effort to use the proper words in conversation. Some of us no longer observe good judgment whether a joke is appropriate or inappropriate for the kind of environment that we are in.

We don't have to make big changes to be 'well-dressed' in our actions and speech. We just have to be more thoughtful and sensitive when we speak.

Coffee and Tea

Let's say you visited my home. I told you that I only had tea to offer. I was glad when you said, "Can you put sugar in it?" instead of, "Can you change it to coffee?"

Adjustment is part and parcel of a thriving relationship. I am willing to accommodate your preference for an addition of sugar to my offer of tea. Seeing you enjoy it will make me feel good. But if I only have tea in my home and you insist that I serve coffee, I would surely resent it.

When others ask a favor from you, say to yourself, "Is it okay with me?"

Small adjustments make you likable. If you bend over backward to make significant sacrifices but resent people in doing so, you will dislike yourself. Your irritation will be evident and people will not like you, either.

The Welcome

The sun comes up in the sky, announcing the start of the day. It goes down at sunset, announcing the end of the day. This precision has been constant for millions of years. The sun's rising and setting does not depend upon anybody's mood. It shines whether people like it or not.

If the sun could speak, it would say that the earth is its favorite rising place. Why? No planet in the solar system welcomes the sun like Earth.

We have roosters, the sun's welcome party. Their cock-a-doodle-doos are unique only to our planet. They greet the sun consistently without being trained to do it.

There are ten people at the nursing station in the psychiatric unit; two are clerks, the rest are nurses.

"Hello, Dr. Malhotra. How are you?" greeted Diane with a beaming smile. She is a nurse who greets me without fail every time I enter the psychiatric unit. I feel very much welcomed as I head toward my patients. If I am the sun, she is the rooster.

We don't need to be hired or assigned the job of smiling, welcoming, and helping others feel light. Greet, smile, and make others feel good whether you are an office clerk, a waiter in a restaurant, or whatever it is that you do.

Be like a rooster. Don't be shy or hesitate to welcome somebody. Who knows? Your greeting may inspire them to have a wonderful day.

Chapter 19:
Pain, Pain, Go Away

Dealing with Chronic Back Pain

Construction workers deal with deafening sounds all day. The volume is high, the pitch is sharp, but they are no longer affected. The noise doesn't give them discomfort.

Why?

They use earplugs or headphones. They're still surrounded by noise, but the reduced loudness causes less pain or discomfort to their eardrums.

Let's use this metaphor for dealing with chronic pain.

The doctor gave you pain medication for your chronic back pain. It offered some relief, but you still felt it all day. It was like a continuous loud noise in the background. It distracted you. You needed earplugs to reduce the impact of pain.

What could be like earplugs to reduce your suffering?

You still have active body faculties. Do volunteer work, a hobby, or a side job. These earplugs will earn you money. Though the pain remains, it will not hurt as intensely.

Why?

The new activities will distract you.

I have worked hard all my life. Taking care of my patients' problems gave me satisfaction and joy. Then I got sick. I sunk into the depths of fear and sadness.

Our mind cannot attend to two things at once. In my case, one choice was to stay on the couch and wallow in self-pity. Another choice was to live and serve.

The second option is better.

Is my tiredness still present? Sure. Chemotherapy drugs cause it.

However, I travel every day to my office. I anticipate seeing my patients. These are my high-quality earplugs that soften the impact of the side-effects.

My 'earplugs' are working.

Choose headphones or earplugs that give you the most efficient filter and distraction from pain.

Island of Distraction

If your motorboat capsized in the middle of a large body of water, the view of a small spot of land would be a very welcome sight indeed. You would swim immediately to it. Living on a small spot of land is not an inviting idea, but it's better than drowning. However, once you have rested, you would go explore. You would look on the horizon for larger islands. When you saw one, you would look for the means to travel there.

I used this metaphor for people who have chronic pain or chronic distress, physical or psychological. Some people have fibromyalgia or chronic joint pain. They say that the pain stays with them 24 hours a day. After a thorough talk, I find that when they are absorbed in a TV show, engrossed in the presence of their visiting grandchildren, or talking with a friend on the phone, they get distracted from the pain. If the pain's intensity was a 10, it was reduced to a 9 or 8.

These are small islands of distraction. It would be possible to find bigger spots of distraction. Fibromyalgia or arthritis will remain, but your quality of life will improve. Why? You have found bigger and better ways of distracting yourself from pain and agony.

Your Mind's Secretary

"I have pain. How can *you* change it?" patients ask me in disbelief.

I tell them the metaphor of the boss and the secretary, which goes like this:

"As I am talking to you now, telephone calls, emails, fax messages, FedEx deliveries, medical representatives, and messages from my family are coming into my office. However, I have instructed my office manager to hold all of them except a phone call from my family. For the next hour, my secretary saves the messages. When you leave, she will give them to me. In short, my manager functions as a gate to control signals according to my instructions."

Let's see how this metaphor applies to pain control.

"Just like I am the boss in my office, the cortex of our brain where our consciousness resides is the boss. Under it is the thalamus. It is the secretary of the cortex. All of the sensations of touching, hearing, seeing, and pain pass through the thalamus before they go to the cortex where the sensations are consciously perceived. The cortex, the boss, tells the thalamus what feelings it wants to address and what feelings it wants to ignore."

I gave multiple examples where a person is distracted from feeling his pain by something that is of great interest to him. Attention to something interesting makes it less severe. However, when he focuses on the pain for whatever reason, it's like ordering his thalamus to send all the pain impulses into his cortex.

Patients to whom I have told this metaphor have recognized that there is a mechanism in their brain by which they can channel the pain and wield some control over it.

Chapter 20:
Overthrowing Fear

Don't Scare the Hell Out of Yourself

Dave came came to me with the somber expression of a man carrying a casket.

"My life is falling apart," he said.

"Have you lost your job?" I asked.

"No."

"Is one of your family members sick?"

"No."

"Financial problems?"

"No."

"Then what makes you say that?"

"The company manager has assigned me a very complicated job."

"Why would that concern you? You are one of their best employees."

"Maybe this is their way of trying to fire me."

"If they want to fire you, they can do it without giving you an important task first. I think they consider you the best man for the job."

"Yes, I think so."

"Do you think you're just scaring yourself?"

"Yes."

"There is no crisis at work. There is only the pressure of the assignment, right?"

"Yes."

"What else is bothering you?"

"My mother is retiring, and she's anxious about the ample time on her hands. She's depressed, but she doesn't go for help."

"Can I speak to your mom?"

"Sure."

Dave dialed a number. "Mom, talk to my doctor," he said and gave the phone to me.

I introduced myself. I told her about Dave's worry. I asked whether she would be interested in seeing a mental health professional.

She agreed. Dave looked relieved. His usual smile appeared.

"When you scare a child by saying, 'Boo!' the child fears without cause. That is exactly what you're doing to yourself."

Don't scare yourself. Look closely at the things that bother you. Then write them down, sort them out, and find solutions for each problem. If you do that consistently, the 'Boos!' have no space in your world.

Talk Yourself Out of Fear

As children, we were afraid of monsters in our closets or under our beds. Our parents used to reassure us, "There's no monster, dear!"

They held our little hands as we all peeked under the bed and into the closets to make sure. At first we were afraid to open our eyes, but they made us do so.

"See? No monster!" they would say.

Facing these places took away our fear. They turned on the light and reassured us once again that there was no monster.

What happened as we were growing up?

We scared ourselves when we encountered problems. The child in us grew more fearful.

However, let us allow the adult in us to take over and reassure the scared child that there are no monsters, and that all of the challenges we face can be overcome.

The Terror Train

Make believe that you're standing on a train track.

Chug.... Chug.... Chug.... A train is coming!

Toot! Toot! You hear its warning whistle.

You see the smoke coming from its chimneys. You feel the tremor of the ground as the train approaches. But you can't move! You're stuck. Terror envelops your whole being.

"I'm so dead," you mumble as you pray.

Did you know that we tend to recreate this same feeling of terror every day?

All of us experience unfortunate incidents in life. Some are out of our control, but some are, unfortunately, *created by us.*

What if they get upset with me because of my action (or inaction)? What if they feel bad because of my decision? What will they say? What will they think of me?

These and many other 'people-pleasing' thoughts are like a train terrorizing you every day.

Get off the track. Let the terror train pass by. Say, "To the best of my understanding and judgment, I will say and do what is fitting. If that's not enough for some people, so be it."

Most of the time you'll discover that your fear is unfounded. It only exists in your own mind. It's not a reality. But if somebody is really sore with you, encourage yourself by saying, "He's only human. There is a limit to what humans can deal with all at once."

Free yourself from the terror train.

The Stake is Good for the Plant

Gina was scared of meeting people. She became anxious whenever she was among them. She had slowly cut off all her ties with the outside world. She was also afraid of going to new places.

Gina had what we call 'social phobia.' Worse, she was also depressed and entertaining thoughts of suicide.

I recommended that she join a meet-up group around her town, so we looked into the directory. I presented them to her one by one.

But her responses were: "I'm not interested in reading books," or, "I'm not into writing," or, "I don't like collecting coins."

I said, "It's not the hobby per se that we are after. I want you to get involved with people and make friends to counter your fear.

"When you want to straighten a little plant, you put a wooden stake next to it to carry the weight of its tender stem. It's the plant that you're interested in, not the stake. You can always get rid of the stake once the plant has grown.

"You are still tender, so we need to put a stake in the form of groups and activities that will make you comfortable around people. Once your fear is gone, you can move away from the groups."

We all need a stake to support our efforts to grow or heal from emotional heaviness.

Chapter 21:
Let Your Marriage Win

Small Defects, Big Problems

There was a distracting sound coming from the rear of your car. You found a loose screw and tightened it. The sound disappeared.

Locating and fixing a small irritation could snuff out a fire that has the potential to spread and destroy. In contrast, an unsolved small situation could balloon into a big issue.

Between husbands and wives, there may be 'small' behaviors or habits that can create difficulties. However, this can be rectified if the couple is communicating well.

Let me tell you about Mr. and Mrs. Patel.

He complained that when he arrived home from work, his wife would stay in the bedroom and not greet him the way she did before.

Mr. Patel had the habit of chewing tobacco.

"Every time he nibbles it, he gets irritable. His irritability bothers me a lot. The smell of tobacco turns me off, too," she complained, "so I hide in our bedroom instead of welcoming him when he arrives at home."

A simple agreement between the couple solved the problem. He agreed to keep the tobacco in his office. By five o'clock, he would take his last dose of it. By six o'clock, he would brush his teeth, gargle, and spray mouth freshener before leaving his office. The tobacco stink became less. The smell no longer bothered his wife. On her part, she agreed to welcome him just like before: with a smile, a hug, a kiss, and endearments like "I missed you. I'm glad you're back."

Two Kinds of Rattlesnakes

There are two kinds of rattlesnakes. One is true to its name; it rattles. The other does not do justice to its name; it is silent.

The population of the 'rattling' snakes is decreasing. They cannot hide for long. They're quickly discovered and killed because of the noise they make.

It isn't known why the second type lost its rattle. Their number is increasing because it's hard to find them. They are more deadly because they are silent. They take people by surprise.

Human beings also fall into one of these categories.

There's no second guessing with some people. You certainly know when they're angry. They cannot help but rattle. They verbalize their emotions. They express their thoughts.

Some people hide their feelings even when they're shaking with anger. They bite their tongues and remain quiet. They withdraw and opt to give others the silent treatment. It's difficult to handle them because you don't know what's going on in their mind.

When your spouse 'rattles,' welcome it. It's easy to avoid her bite because you know where she stands. Knowing her mind is an effective way to help manage her anger. Welcoming your spouse's rattling is your way of appreciating her being open with you.

Do Not Personalize It

"I'm maturing emotionally with age. I'm no longer super sensitive. I've stopped criticizing my husband," Marian said.

"If he didn't eat what I cooked, I used to say, 'You only want what your mother cooks.' If we were at a party, I would fight and say, 'How come you're so hungry today?' All of that is history. When the same thing happens today, I just shrug my shoulders and think, 'He's not eating because he's not hungry.' I've stopped thinking that I'm a bad cook," she explained further.

In Marian's earlier years, her self-concept and confidence were low. She carried her insecurities into her marriage. She would take on every perceived response her husband gave her as something she was doing wrong.

106

Today, she's no longer interpreting her husband's actions as her own personal failure. In effect, her husband is happy that Marian has become less critical of every little thing he does. He loves it.

I Changed Jobs

Nicole's husband developed aplastic anemia. He had to visit his hematologist and the hospital for blood transfusions. He needed a lot of help.

With this development, Nicole felt that her dream was 'sabotaged' by her husband's illness. She had to quit her job. She had long been looking forward to retiring and traveling, so she resented being stuck at his bedside. She was angry at their situation, but she felt guilty at the same time because she loved her husband.

"Change how you look at your current station in life. This is your only recourse to free yourself from condemnation," I told her.

"Repeatedly say to yourself, 'I have *not* quit my job. I'm just changing jobs from a salesperson to a nursing assistant.'

"To counter your impatience every time you help your husband, say, 'I'm on nursing duty. I'm saving $600 per day.'" (If she were to hire a caregiver, she would be paying $25 an hour.)

Changing her frame of mind about her husband's illness and her caregiving duties slowly freed Nicole from her frustrations. She is now content with serving her husband as a nursing assistant. Her positive outlook defeated her negative emotions.

Request Instead of Complaining

"Your face looks like your sister's," Sylvia's husband said.

"Why don't you appreciate me anymore? Why don't you say that I look good instead of criticizing me? Why do you keep on complaining about my looks?" Sylvia yelled.

"This is why I don't open my mouth: because you always yell at me," her husband responded.

They angrily turned their backs on each other. The bedroom became as silent as a mausoleum.

Sylvia missed being appreciated and praised, but she made one mistake: she demanded it by complaining, "Why don't you…?"

Complaining? Yes. Whenever somebody uses that phrase, it becomes a complaint, and it's very hard to praise somebody who is grumbling.

Now, how about the following?

"Honey, you used to whisper 'sweet nothings' to me. Can I have a dose of that today?"

"Love, you used to slap my behind and say, 'You are damn sexy.' I miss it. Please keep doing what makes me feel good."

A request touches the emotions more than complaints do. In addition, it makes the other person feel needed, and that is a very good thing.

Unlearn the bad habit of complaining; learn the art of requesting.

Me or Your Mother

Your wife jolted you by asking, "Who is your favorite, your mother or me?"

You reacted with a squirm, then a quiet smile, then a joke that you thought would let you 'escape' without causing a storm. But it didn't work.

I suggest that you say, "If you love me, you won't have me choose between two important people in my life. It's like asking me which one of my eyes is more necessary, the left or the right. It's like telling me to lose an eye that I love. Do I love my right eye more than the other or vice versa? No. I need both my eyes for depth perception."

This answer will satisfy a mentally healthy spouse. But not all spouses are that healthy.

An argument may occur because of insecurity and jealousy. During moments like these, people tend to ask things that they don't apply to themselves, like an ultimatum: "Choose: me or your mother!"

A proposition like this puts you at a crossroads. Either way, you lose. Fear of losing your wife may push you to say, "You." Then you will be eaten up with guilt about your mother. If you say, "Mother," you will injure your wife's ego and all hell may break loose.

How do you treat this delicate question?

The answer was best given by one of my patients.

On their wedding day, his wife asked him, "Who is more important, your mother or me?"

He had faced lots of difficulties with his mother, yet his answer was, "Don't ask that question again. Anyone who asks me that will not like the answer."

Notice that my patient did not name his choice. It was a wise reply to a silly, problematic question that didn't deserve an answer.

If you say, "You are more important," it will haunt you every time she has you choose again between her and anyone else. Her reminder will always be, "You promised me."

Naming names in response to this question is like jumping into a trap. Therefore, refuse to jump into it.

Now... excuse me. Are you the the person who is *asking* this kind of question?

Deal with Crises in a Relationship

Three-year-old kids are distracted by candies, toys, or being sleepy. They express their needs with a request, a threat, or crying.

"I don't love Mommy anymore. I'm going away to live with Grandma," they declare. They are young, so you deal with them patiently.

Some spouses are like three-year-old kids. Beer or TV distract a husband, so he fails to cut the lawn or wash the dishes.

You feel like you have another kid. Your wife wants to buy things that the budget won't allow. She's irritable, tired, and premenstrual. You feel like you have an additional teenage daughter.

You have been dealing well with your three-year-old kid. You don't panic at his threat of leaving. You pacify him with, "Daddy and Mommy love you so much."

At the end of the day, you're able to put him in bed and kiss him goodnight. He wakes up in the morning fresh, his demands completely forgotten.

When your angry spouse announces his or her decision to leave, the three-year-old has emerged. But you get scared. You forget to handle his or her inner child in a low-key manner like you did with your kid.

Keep your wits about you. Don't be shaken by your spouse's threat. Deal with it calmly. Maintain your poise.

If they persist in saying, "I'm going to divorce you," a wise answer would be, "I love you; I don't want a divorce. I will do whatever it takes to save our marriage. But if that's what makes you happy, you are free to do so."

You survived before you met him or her, you will survive after they leave.

Continue this kind of inner talk. It will produce tranquility. It will show in your demeanor. Seeing your coolness, your spouse will most likely settle down and work out the issues with you.

Dancing and Stepping on Toes

Imagine that we were dancing and I kept stepping on your toes. I apologized every time you said, "Ouch!"

I told you about my hip problem, but I knew you would be fed up with my apologies. You would refuse to dance with me the next time I asked.

Having justifiable reasons for hurting others does not take away the pain. Find ways to rectify the problem.

In my case, I should have stopped dancing and just been content with sitting and watching. If I really wanted to dance, I should have gotten my hip treated first.

How does this apply to relationships?

Rebecca came to me with a problem: chronic depression and too much work around the house.

"They left me no time and energy for my husband," she said. "I always tell him my reasons when he complains."

The couple would always end up arguing. Her husband would stomp off into the living room and make the sofa his bed. On the other hand, Rebecca would feel justified.

Justifying herself did not solve her problem, it only explained her refusal. The problem, if left unattended, would create serious trouble in her marriage even though it was not her fault.

Rebecca did most of the housework in the afternoon, and she was exhausted by evening. She could do the bulk of the work in the morning. She could get her depression treated. She could hire household help.

Don't just explain away your problem. In the end, only solutions matter because only solutions work.

The Audio System of Emotions and Behavior

Author's note: I'm not sure whether I read this metaphor somewhere and just revised it, but I have frequently used it since the 90's, so I lost track. Hence, if anyone discovers that there is an original author of it, please let me know. I will be happy to give full credit where credit is due.

There are three controls in an audio system: volume, bass, and treble. By sliding the knobs up and down, you can create a sound that fits your preference.

There are also three controls in a relationship.

There is *frequency*. How many times do you meet, play, do things together, or go on vacation together? How many times do you correspond or talk on the phone or via text messages, letters, and emails?

There is *duration*. When you meet, is it an hour-long conversation or a full weekend of being together?

There is *intensity*. What do you say and do, and how do you say and do these things? Are you passive even though everybody is frantic about the stock market? Do you scream your frustrations about the ineptness of government officials? Does your pleasure not only make you smile but make you bake a cake? Are you active or laid back with your concerns?

A patient of mine was a divorced man. He married again. His young wife had a 13-year-old daughter of her own. He participated in the girl's care. He treated her like his very own.

The daughter, now 17 years old, knocked on the door at 2:30 in the morning. He opened the door.

"This is not an appropriate time to come home," he said.

"F--- off! Don't tell me what to do. You're not my father," she answered back.

"Okay, suit yourself," he said.

The next day, she said, "Can you drop me off at my friend's house?"

He said, "I'm not your father, remember? Call your father and let him do it."

She went crying to her mother, who got very angry. The couple's conflict concerning her daughter put their marriage on the brink of breaking.

I said, "You're living under one roof, so the frequency and duration of meeting and talking is difficult to control, but cutting down on the intensity is very possible.

"She is not your daughter. You don't have to take an 'active' role in molding her to be a 'good girl.' Let her mother take the lead when it comes to the girl's discipline."

From then on, he participated in everything except telling her what and what not to do. Things went back to normal.

You don't have to switch off the sound. In the same way, you don't have to cut off your important relationships. You can simply increase or decrease the frequency, duration, and intensity of your involvement based on what you want to accomplish in that relationship.

Who Gets Along?

Some examples of complimentary couples could be:
- talker, listener
- good cook, good eater
- leader, follower
- one person the mothering and fathering kind, the other is dependent
- initiator, follower

Some couples are similar to each other in most things. They appreciate each other because of shared interests, like my wife and I who have the same passion for action, dogs, movies, and our love for our children.

Getting along with your spouse has nothing to do with personality. Differing and similar personalities may or may not fulfill each other's needs. Habits like bringing up mistakes of the past, disrespecting the spouse in front of people, disagreement with money spending, and misuse of time are some of the top culprits in most conflicts, not the differences or similarities in personality.

Think of clothes. Some people have the same color trousers and jackets. Some always wear similar suits. Other people mix and match clothes and colors, like blue with red, green with blue, earth colors with yellow, neutral colors with dark colors, and others. There are combinations that are elegant and cool. There are combinations that make you squirm in distaste. A rainbow in the sky will drive us to say "Wow!" A rainbow combination in clothing will drive us to say "What?!"

Some habits don't mix well in some marriages. Sooner or later, people get tired of binge drinking, drugs, compulsive gambling, extra-marital affairs, or imbalanced behavior.

Examine the habits that create difficulties in your relationship. You can curb them without worrying about your individual personalities. Clothes can be mixed and matched when there is a desire to dress well. Different personalities can be mixed and matched when there is a mutual desire to make the relationship last longer.

The Airy Spouse

I am fond of hats. I have Indian, Italian, Arabic, and American hats. Of all the hats I have, I am most fond of wearing a hat made of straw. Compared to the rest it's inexpensive, but I always end up wearing it.

Why did that hat become my favorite?

First, it looks good on me and I get many compliments. Second, it's light. I often forget that I have it on my head. It feels like I have next to nothing on my head. I have to take off the other hats because my head feels tight, sweaty, and hot. There is airflow through the straw hat. It keeps my head cool in hot weather and warm in cold weather.

A husband and wife should be like my straw hat. He is supposed to not only 'decorate' his spouse's life with money and jewelry, but also appreciate her to make her feel good inside. They serve each other's needs. There is a flow of ideas between them. They graciously welcome each other's friends into their lives.

Once the relationship is on a less constricted level, each partner becomes like my straw hat.

Keeper or Cheaper

A bundle of sticks remains intact depending on the strength of the string that binds them together. A marriage needs strings to keep it together.

Some societies reserve sex for wedlock. It results in interdependence for sexual fulfillment.

In some households, when the wife does not cook, the husband goes hungry. When the husband doesn't bring in money, the wife goes hungry. The interdependence serves as a strong string.

In industrial societies, most couples work. The wife stops depending on her husband for money; the man stops expecting his wife to cook. This has weakened the strings of marriage. The couples quickly press the 'break up' button after a trivial argument.

I want you to know that there is one divorce law that may serve as a strong string that will keep the sticks of marriage intact. The law rules that the spouse who has money is required to transfer half of his earnings into the pocket of the spouse who has less. In other words, a $60K family will suddenly become two $30K households in the event of a divorce. In this case, a partner could choose to be a 'keeper' of the marriage, or live a 'cheaper' life through divorce.

Every time you are tempted to learn more about the divorce option, ask yourself, "Am I going to be happier? Am I going to be richer? Am I going to have more company in the evening? Could it be better if I put some hard work into my present relationship rather than divorcing and starting over, facing new sets of problems including financial stress?"

Choose what you would rather be, a keeper or a cheaper.

Don't Trade Gold for Brass

Your 22-karat gold ring looked ordinary. As years went by, you became bored with wearing it. You replaced it with a cheap but flashy imitation. You liked its flare, so you wore the flashy one on your nights out. However, when you got home, you took it off your finger and put your gold ring on again.

If you get bored with something of value, you will probably get bored with the cheap one after some time, too. You would rather lose the imitation than the original, though, right?

Your 22-karat family and friends may be less impressive and exciting than an imitation person seems. It's possible that the sexy secretary in your office is trying to attract you. However, once you've had your fling, you will soon realize that you exchanged your real jewelry for a worthless imitation, which does not last long.

Likes and Dislikes

I like shrimp; my wife likes chicken. I like to end dinner with a fruit; she likes chocolate. When I offer her fruit, she refuses; when she offers me chocolate, I refuse.

She feels hot at 72 degrees; I feel cold and shivery. I want her to enjoy different pieces of jewelry; she wants to wear the same locket. She is a homebody and I love to initiate outside contacts and maintain them.

We love our little dog named Toofy; love our two sets of parents; love our sons, daughters-in-law, and grandchildren. We are both psychiatrists, and we love our profession. In our practice, I manage public relations and she takes care of the finances.

When she rejects something from me, I don't take it as disrespect or indifference toward me. I don't see her ways as a negation of my personality.

She has the same outlook.

There are differences and similarities. I call them 'positive' because our relationship is able to stand the test of time. They bind us together; we have grown stronger.

Disliking things does not mean disliking each other. The same is true with colleagues, siblings, parents and children, and religions. When we see our likes and dislikes as differences of opinion rather than the 'superiority' of one over the other, relationships flourish. But when people look down on each other's differences or feel threatened by the other person's negation, a dialog is in order so that peace and understanding prevail.

New Restaurant, Old Taste

You went to a new Chinese restaurant and ordered pork fried rice, fish with pepper sauce, and shrimp Hunan style. As you ate, you kept on comparing the taste of the food to another restaurant. Two dishes were tasty, and one was less tasty than those in the other restaurant.

"This is not a good restaurant," you concluded. You were evaluating the new restaurant with your old taste.

It's unfair to write off a restaurant after tasting three dishes from a menu of 300, isn't it?

This is like a marriage. After a while, you start comparing your wife to other women in terms of habits, clothing style, looks, how she talks, and how she treats you.

You have not lived with the other woman, have not slept with her, and have not related to her as a mother of your children. You have not tasted the whole menu of the other woman's behavior, attitude, and value system for a just comparison.

Keep an open mind about your spouse's contribution to your family. Look at yourself also. You are an imperfect human being, and so is your spouse. A little positive here and a little negative there are realities for all couples.

A talk with your spouse could take care of a lack of spice in the relationship. Small adjustments here and there can make both of you happy.

Remember: You are an imperfect couple... and so are all others.

Deflated

You were stranded on a highway because you neglected to check the tire pressure. You had to call a tow truck to fix the tires.

During routine maintenance, inflating a car tire takes minutes. On the highway, it ate four hours of your time due to additional hassles.

Your spouse is like the car tires that carry a lot of burden. Though you are the driver who is putting money on the table, your wife is taking care of unending hassles. If you cut her down and find fault with her cooking, child-care, the laundry, and the cleanliness of the house, it's like sucking the air out of her self-esteem.

On the other hand, expressing your praise and appreciation would inflate her sense of pride. A spouse who doesn't hear words of encouragement is like a deflated tire. A deflated wife could easily break down under small pressures in finances or in the relationship. A deflated sense of pride cannot bear family strains for long.

Criticizing your wife for being weak is like kicking the tire that went flat. In reality, you could prevent it by inflating her ego through words of encouragement, recognition, appreciation, and praise.

You check your car's air pressure from time to time. To avoid hassles, do the same for your spouse's self-esteem. This doesn't only apply to wives, either; it also applies vice versa.

Driving with Tunnel Vision

Ben was a successful lawyer. He had visited Los Angeles seven times in the last 15 years. He would fly on a Sunday night, arrive Monday morning, and go to client meetings. Around 4:30 the same afternoon, he would fly back to New Jersey.

Recently, he discovered that Dan, a colleague, had been bringing his family along on his business trips. Dan would go one day early and stay one day longer. He took his family on excursions and sightseeing. He was a competent lawyer who simultaneously enjoyed life with his family.

Ben wondered, "Why haven't I done the same thing?"

He quickly realized the answer. He remembered that while he was a student, studying was the only thing he knew. He thought that he would fail in achieving his goals if he goofed off. His habit of 'all work and no play' had stayed with him despite his established career.

Ben had achieved his goals and it was time for him to relax. He decided to do what Dan did. He asked about places to visit in Los Angeles and bought first-class tickets for his wife and children.

Ben was like a driver who traveled from home to work every day. On both sides of the highway was lush greenery, but he didn't see it. He was focused on the concrete road, constantly lost in thought about strategies for solving his cases.

He discussed it with his wife. They planned to take regular mini-vacations to avoid burning out—Ben as a lawyer, his wife as a homemaker.

The Spices of a Real Partnership

Do similarities or dissimilarities attract and keep people together?

I've heard that people get along because of dissimilarities. For example, Ace is a quiet man who listens. His wife, Joanne, is a perpetual talker. Joanne talks, Ace listens. She likes to cook; he does not know what garlic looks like. He likes good food; she feels proud when he appreciates her cooking. Everything is well in their camp.

Another argument is that people get along well with each other because of their similarities.

I like a dachshund dog; my wife likes the same. We share lots of laughter and bonding time playing with our dog. If she liked cats and I hated cats, we would not be having fun 'together' with our pets. Would such a dissimilarity create a problem between us?

Both of us like reading and watching historical movies. This causes us to be 'one' in enjoying the same stuff. If she liked something but I did not, I wouldn't participate in those hobbies with her. Would the dissimilarity create a problem between us?

Look at daal chawal (lentils and rice), bread and butter, or steak and potatoes. They are not similar, but the combination makes the dinner complete to the diners' satisfaction.

No two people are perfectly the same in their preferences and attitudes. Differences will always be present. The question isn't whether similarity and dissimilarity bring harmony in the relationship. The real question is: are two people preparing their similarities and differences with the 'spices' of mutual respect and negotiation?

Simply put, similarities and dissimilarities don't count much unless the spices of mutual respect and peaceful negotiation don't complement them.

Put the Hammer Away

Debbie had multiple arguments with her husband.

"He's furious. He said I'm flirting with other men," she said.

"Is the accusation true?" I asked.

"Yes," she answered after a few seconds of silence.

"What's your reason for doing it?"

"I don't mean any harm. It was nothing serious, just a little fun for me," she explained.

"Why is that?"

"One, it makes me feel I'm still attractive. Two, in case my husband leaves me, I already have a few people lined up. But I don't have extramarital affairs."

Flirting is a tool that single people employ in finding mates.

Has your purpose been achieved? If yes, then stop it; otherwise, the tool that helped you in the past will become the very tool that makes you lose what you worked for in the first place.

Carpenters use a hammer to attach panels of wood. When construction is done, there's no need to hit the painted, decorated walls with the hammer. Its force will leave an ugly dent or hole in the immaculate walls.

Put the hammer of flirting away. It will just ruin the walls of your marriage.

Hobbies as a Cause of Disagreements

We need interests or hobbies as a breather from work. However, a hobby may become the source of irritation or arguments between couples. Here are two examples of hobbies that caused some problems.

One spouse's pastime is watching TV or spending time on the internet. Night after night, the other spouse would wait up late into the night, and would often fall asleep while waiting.

Furniture-making is the husband's hobby. The wife had requested that the husband get a gallon of milk three times. The man was so engrossed in what he was doing that it was hard for him to detach himself from it. The wife was growing grouchier by the minute as she waited for him to go to the store.

In the first example, the subject neglected his/her spousal responsibility. TV-watching was interfering with their intimacy. In the second example, the subject neglected trivial but necessary functions. Spouses are not saints; they blow up when pushed to the edge.

The hobby itself doesn't cause problems; your handling of your hobby does.

Disengage yourself from your hobby when needed. Take care of the family's needs first and return to it later. Your hobby is not going to get hurt or complain, but your spouse will. Give priority to your spouse, and your hobby will never become the source of trouble.

Chapter 22:
Reciprocal Persistence and Patience

Light at the End of the Tunnel

Tunnels play their own important part in the plans of a city. They support infrastructures and sewage systems.

People who work in tunnels spend their working hours in darkness with some electric lights guiding their way. They come out tired and weary, with soiled and muddy work clothes. The larger and more significant the project is, the longer their working hours below ground are. Without these 'mud diggers,' our transportation system would be completely outdated, which would mean a lot of extra travel time for commuters. After many months, they reach the specified end of the project and see the light at the end of the tunnel.

Let's say that you're working at a job that seems insignificant and that you don't enjoy. Day after day, dragging your feet and feeling rotten, you work in a half-lit basement office. Your two sons' education pushes you to trudge along.

When your older son finally got his engineering diploma, it was like getting out of the long tunnel and taking a break from the mud to inhale fresh air. It made your next load lighter.

Then the time came for your younger son to graduate in medicine. Relatives, friends, and colleagues congratulated you. Again, you saw the bright lights at the end of the tunnel.

Some important projects in life test our patience. They require a longer time to accomplish. One thing is sure, though: All your hard work becomes worthwhile when you finally see the light at the end of the tunnel, the fruits of your labor.

No Effort Goes Unrewarded

I misplaced my eyeglasses. It created difficulty for me because I could not read small print. I searched everywhere in the house and couldn't find them. Instead, I found 12 handkerchiefs that had been missing for two years. My past searches were futile, so I had given up on them. I also found $15 worth of loose change.

Simply put, the exercise of searching for solutions to a problem will never be wasted. Your search may not solve your original problem, but there could be 'incidental' solutions to long-standing issues that may pleasantly surprise you.

The combination of effort and patience pays off.

When the Buck Stops with You

Dave was sweating profusely. He was working on an old, rusty garden hose. He tried for about 15 minutes before giving up.

"What are you going to do?" his father asked upon seeing Dave stretching up and heaving a sigh. He was sitting in a chair on their lawn.

"I'll call a plumber," Dave answered.

"What will the plumber do?"

"He'll do the same thing that I did. He'll just work at it until he fixes it because he's getting paid."

"Well, make believe that you're the plumber. You've got to do it because you can't get another plumber to work on it," his father encouraged.

Dave went back and started working on the hose again. Before long, he was able to fix it.

Persistence

The handle of my bedroom door was loose. I adjusted the screws, but it didn't work.

"Work a little more on it," my brother instructed, "because there's no reason the screw shouldn't tighten."

I went back and tried again. I got the same result.

My brother came over and worked on the handle using the same screwdriver. He took a long time.

As I watched, it seemed to me that the screw was turning without getting any grip inside. As I thought about getting a new handle, *click!* The screw gripped something inside. The handle was tight again.

"There was nothing wrong with your approach. You just didn't persist long enough," my brother said.

Oftentimes, people start with half-hearted effort like I did with the handle.

There's no reason why you can't get a grip on the 'inside' of a problem if you persist. So don't quit your job, business, project, or relationships. There will be a point when you hear that *click.*

This is My Turn

A prolonged illness becomes stressful for most family members. It's easy to take care of a loved one's fever for a few days, but beyond those days, it becomes hard for the caregivers, especially in severe cases of chronic illness. A storm of love, affection, exhaustion, anger, irritability, and guilt rushes in. It starts to wrench the human spirit, causing despair and burnout.

During my father-in-law's last years in life, he developed mild dementia and agitation. He would always say, "It's better to go now."

Looking after him was difficult. He kept getting out of bed. My mother-in-law cared for him like a devoted nun. She didn't complain or show annoyance.

"Mummy, where do you get this patience from?" I asked her one day.

"He took care of me all my life. Now it's my turn," she answered.

We requested that she move in with us after my father-in-law passed away.

Years passed by. During the last year of my mother-in-law's life, she had multiple complications and was hospitalized several times, which consumed all of our time and energy.

As I came out from her hospital room to sit on a bench, I remembered her statement: "He took care of me all my life. Now it's my turn."

My memory of her commitment soothed my tired mind, emotions, and body. Mummy had lovingly taken care of my wife all her life. It was our turn to take care of Mummy.

Snowballing Relationships

How is an avalanche of snow and ice formed? It usually starts with something small.

Let's suppose it's snowing. A branch falls to the ground. The impact disturbs and pushes the precariously stacked ice and snow under the tree. The force has a domino effect, moving and pushing other mounds down the slope. On its way down, it gathers more and more snow, ice, and debris. As a result, it becomes stronger and stronger. It finally hits bottom, destroying everything in its path.

Almost all siblings have problems during childhood. The younger ones are the most vulnerable. They have a sense of inferiority as they see the abilities and competence of their older siblings.

This problem can also occur between cousins or friends.

A small reproof or an unintentional snub may be taken seriously by a child. As time passes by, disagreements with other children or reproofs from other adults in the family can increase the perception of unfair treatment. The resulting hurt could cause his relationship with his sibling or cousin to be uneasy and contentious as he grows up.

The hostilities can be stopped when someone recognizes the snowballing or avalanche effect that's happening.

What was the event during childhood that became the seed for the current uneasy relationship? Was it a bike broken by the cousin who never said sorry or got it repaired? Was it a plastic bucket borrowed and never returned? Many small things could be the cause.

When a person recognizes that a past childhood 'sin' is the cause of the present relationship between him and the other party, he may start to respond with understanding and calm. Only a patient and loving response from the 'enlightened' person will make the other party respond in kind.

Chapter 23:
Onward to Your Full Potential

Ignite Your Matchstick

Matchsticks are imprisoned in a small box without light or space. But when a hand picks one out and strikes it to the surface of the box, it suddenly sparks to life. The matchstick that had been lying in the dark suddenly lights up.

We are the same. We go to work, return home, watch TV, eat, and go to bed. We meet friends, share jokes, laugh, and drink the same beer. None of these everyday routines are challenging. We are dormant when we're in a cozy and undemanding environment. Our creative energy is locked inside the 'matchstick comfort zone.'

Then we happen to interact with someone at a new company, a party, a seminar, or in a lecture room. Our desire to achieve more is suddenly stirred up. We light up like a matchstick.

You need to meet people who give you fresh perspectives and appreciation for life. These kind of people will infuse a hunger in you to aim higher and achieve. They motivate you to read newspapers, inspire you to get out, embolden you to talk to people, and provoke you to discover. They discuss things unknown to you. They scratch at buried inspiration in you. They strengthen your belief in yourself.

Soon I hope to see you burning brighter and lighting up all of your relationships.

Become Interesting

I want to become an interesting person. How do I become one?

Easy! Get genuinely interested in the people and things around you.

Let's say you take your girlfriend out. As soon as you meet her, close your eyes, take a deep breath, and say, "You smell divine. What are you wearing today?"

Instead of dropping in at your usual hangout, you could try a new restaurant or café that you haven't tried before.

You look at the menu with great interest. When you order, you say to the waiter, "I would like to have this steak done medium rare. Make sure the chef removes the fat from the sides and adds a little Worcestershire sauce." After ordering, let your girlfriend talk about everything that she wants to talk about.

Are you an interesting person? Sure you are. There are millions of things in this vast universe that you can take an interest in. The list is infinite.

You don't have to be doing things with people for them to become interested in you. Taking an interest in them will do the job.

A Fresh Breath of Air

We need oxygen to live. We don't need a license or a permit to breathe. You can even condition your lungs by learning the yogic methods of breathing.

Positive attitude is all around us like oxygen. Exposing ourselves to confident people and imitating their habits is like inhaling clean air.

You don't have to ask anybody's permission to take a new approach.

Has anybody ever asked you, "Why are you breathing fresh air?"

In the same way, nobody has the right to grumble and complain, "Why are you learning by going to college?" or, "Why are you trying to form a new habit to better yourself?"

Overwhelmed

I was juggling two balls. I had seen someone do it at a party. The balls kept falling. I was overwhelmed, so I stopped trying.

I went to YouTube on my computer to see how it was done. The instructions were: (1) Start with one ball. (2) Increase the number of balls when you become an expert with two. (3) Juggle five balls without any problem. (4) Smile and talk while juggling.

I was serious about learning. I started with one ball. I was so focused I forgot to blink.

Whew! I still had a hard time. On the other hand, the man in the video looked like he could juggle five balls while sleeping.

The things you do in life like office work, housework, being a wife, taking care of children, and going to the market are like juggling balls. In the beginning, everything seems difficult. You feel overwhelmed. But you know you will learn with practice.

There was never a problem with the balls. The problem was with my ability to juggle them.

Whenever you're stressed about doing something, ask yourself, "Where can I learn a technique, system, or strategy to juggle better and faster?"

Recognize your lack of skills. Research and learn from the experts. Then become an expert yourself.

Become a Hydroplane

The storm was strong. The sea was rough and tough. A boat was tossed to and fro by the strong waves. If a boat or a yacht had wings, it could fly like a hydroplane and escape the raging seas.

Rocco was a worker in a large factory. He witnessed a co-worker being crushed by a machine. Flashbacks of the accident terrorized him every time he entered the factory. He had nightmares, severe anxiety attacks, and he developed post-traumatic stress disorder. His workplace had become a storm of torment. But what could he do? He needed his job.

Rocco loved boating. He had been wanting to buy a yacht, but he couldn't own one unless he got a captain's license. He decided to get the necessary training.

After he got the training he needed, he left his old job because his license had gotten him a well-paying new job.

Rocco's nerves were almost destroyed. His life was slowly sinking, but with the extra education he acquired, his boat had developed wings. He flew and escaped.

Whenever you feel like you're drowning, ask yourself, "What wings of new skills or new hobbies can I develop so I can fly toward new jobs? What wings of attitude can I develop so I can fly toward new relationships?"

A Strong Hand to Support the Weak Hand

Our body has two sides, left and right. A person would use his healthy arm to massage his other arm that has developed some weakness. The strong hand supports and revives the ailing arm.

In the same way, your sagging morale can be helped by an active, sharp mind.

Our thoughts come and go, and some are self-defeating. Activate your rational mind to bring strength and stability. If you don't feel like studying, talk to that sluggish part. Say, "You can do it. Rise because your future and your ability to earn a living depend upon it."

Fools Believe Tools are the Answer

"Every letter is like a pearl and every sentence a pearl necklace."

My mother's description of Pramod's handwriting fit to a T. He was my classmate in eighth grade. He had beautiful calligraphy-like penmanship. Mine was irregular, uneven, and illegible.

A fountain pen has a writing point called a nib, a metal point with a capillary channel. It's mounted on a wooden holder. I found out the secret of Pramod's handwriting: his nib in the holder was soft. Mine was hard.

"If you give me your nib, I will give you four paisas. You can buy a new nib," I proposed to him one day. A nib cost one paisa then.

Pramod came from a poor family, so I was sure the money would be irresistible. He hesitated. I understood why. He had seasoned his nib with months of writing. However, I persisted in badgering him until he gave in and walked away with his prized nib.

I started to write, confident that my handwriting would now be similar to Pramod's. To my dismay, my penmanship remained as it was—ugly. I was mistaken in believing that the tool was the answer. I thought it was more important than having the skill. Pramod wrote beautifully because he was careful and cautious as he wrote.

Skill is primary; tools are secondary.

Most of us have dozens of unread books on our bookshelves. Some of us have unopened toolboxes. In contrast, I have a friend who makes beautiful pieces of furniture and does home repairs with one small toolbox.

A combination of desire, skill, persistence, and hard work is the firepower to success. Focus on developing your skills.

Three Choices

In the struggle of living, there are always three choices:
(1) Give up.
(2) Run away.
(3) Fight.
If you are in the water, you can do three things:
(1) Give up swimming, drown, and die.
(2) Get out of the water, run, and never come back.
(3) Recognize that water is part of life and learn to swim.
In coping with marriage, education, work, relationships, money management, drinking, eating, or gambling, you have three choices:
(1) You drown in your problem and finish yourself in it.
(2) You remove yourself from the scene. Divorce your wife, quit your job, or stop your schooling.

(3) You recognize the difficulty as a lack of problem-solving skills on your part. You educate yourself, learn new skills, and move on.

Chapter 24:
All in a Day's Work

Organizational Squabbles

Squabbles, power struggles, politics. Daphne is sick and tired of problems in the company where she works. She wants to quit and look for another job.

When you enter a big factory, you hear the different sounds of various machines. Some are moving, some are cutting, and some are grinding. Some sounds are piercing; you have to cover your ears. Some are no big deal; they are tolerable. Some are just a whirr; they don't disturb anyone.

A large organization is like a big factory. What you're seeing and hearing are normal corporate sounds and scenes. Learn to cover your ears and eyes. Learn to shrug your shoulders and say, "No bother... no worries." Read literature on how to maneuver your way through the ins and outs of the corporate world. Educate yourself about common office issues. Becoming an expert in dealing with squabbles, power struggles, and politics is the way to survive without being corrupted and burned.

Joyful Hard Work

The keyboard produced melody at the touch of the organist's expert fingers. His well-chosen music floated through the air. I saw people tapping their hands on their stomachs. Some tapped their toes on the floor to the rhythm.

This happened whenever the musician came to play for the cancer patients in the chemotherapy room.

After two hours of playing, he packed up the massive keyboard. He lifted it up and laid it in its case. He closed the huge case securely and placed it on a small cart. Then he put the keyboard stand on his shoulder.

That was a lot of work!

He turned to all of us, smiled, said goodbye, and walked out the door.

I pictured him coming to the hospital from his home. He lifted the huge instrument and its stand, left his house, and put them in his car. Upon reaching the hospital, he opened the trunk of his car and took out the small cart. Next, he lifted up the massive case and settled it in the cart. Then he picked up the keyboard stand and rested it on his shoulder. He maneuvered his way to the hospital building and through doors and elevators. Reaching the chemotherapy room, he put the stand in the middle of the room, opened the case, and set up the instrument on the stand.

That was a lot of work, too!

The man comes to play in the chemotherapy room twice a week. He does not receive a single cent from the hospital. He offers his musical skill for charity.

Listening to his music was a joyful distraction while the chemicals were being pumped through our veins. As the music hovered in the air, it felt like I was flying over lush greenery. I forgot my pain for the time being.

His choice of music was evidently a product of careful selection. His playing was clearly the fruit of persistent practice. Add to that his efforts in going back and forth from the hospital. The musician gave us joy; his was hard work done with joy.

A Rock in the Middle of the Floor

Margo did not get along with her supervisor.

"He's always criticizing me in front of others. He loves to humiliate me," she said.

She went home in a foul mood every day. She vented her frustration to her husband and kids.

It's like she has a huge rock in the middle of her living room. Each time she walks by, she stubs her toe on it.

She stands there crying, "I got hurt again. I have bad luck."

Her husband told her to throw the rock outside, but she ignored the advice.

Margo has to recognize that words, no matter how high-pitched, will not move the rock out of her living room. Complaining, cursing, and yelling will only become habits that don't solve anything. She has to act: move the rock to a corner or throw it out of the house.

What does that mean?

She can visit the human resources department of her company and request a transfer to another department, or she can eject the nasty supervisor out of her life by changing her job.

Is there a rock in your life that you always stub your toes on? Is there somebody you are complaining about? Is it something that has been going on for months, but you have not taken a definitive step to solve it? Does your complaining spoil your mood and everybody else's around you?

Examine what the 'rocks' are. Ponder how to get them out before they damage the peace in your home. Then take clear, decisive action.

Positive Reward Conditioning

'Positive' means a pleasing thing like food. 'Reward' is something you give in response to an action. 'Conditioning' means creating a new habit.

My doggie used to discharge inside the house. But for a long time now, he has been doing it in the yard. We trained him through positive reward conditioning.

Keep a treat like a biscuit or a piece of cheese in your pocket. Go to the yard with your dog. Don't interact much with him. Just watch carefully. When he pees or poops, immediately say, "Good boy, good boy!" then feed him with what you have. It serves as a positive reward for good behavior. The more he gets a positive reward in the yard, the less he goes inside the house.

Positive reward conditioning is deliberate.

How can you use positive reward conditioning in your relationships?

I hired a secretary who was recommended by a friend. I noticed that Liza did not communicate with my patients in the waiting room. She didn't smile, offer coffee or tea, or do anything to make my patients feel welcome.

A couple of patients commented that the previous manager was splendid, though they didn't say anything against the present one.

Liza had worked in the back office of a large corporation doing accounting work. She had no experience interacting with clients.

I started to train Liza similarly to how I trained my dog.

Unbeknownst to her, I was observing her. One day, I saw her smile while she talked. When the patient left, I immediately approached her and said, "That was beautiful, Liza."

She asked, "What was beautiful?"

"I saw you smiling at Mr. and Mrs. Williams. You have a beautiful smile," I explained.

From then on, I noticed that she smiled more frequently.

One day, I saw her giving a glass of water to a patient in the waiting room. After the patient's session with me, I called her to my office.

"Mrs. Jackson said that you are a great secretary," I said.

Her eyes lit up as she asked, "What did she say?"

"She said that you offered her a glass of cold water. She felt welcome in our office," I explained.

Liza started interacting positively with all my patients. Each time I witnessed it, I always verbalized my appreciation.

Within six months, Liza blossomed. She had added warm social interaction to her efficiency. She turned out to be one of the best secretaries I had ever hired. The path to her social skill development came solely through appreciation and gratitude from her employer. She never heard any criticism from me.

Look at someone in your life. Recognize his deficient behavior. Watch him carefully until he makes an affirmative action. Then shower him with praise.

Do it repeatedly. You will see a miracle happen.

Retreat to Win

Emily is a competent supervisor. She gets along well with her colleagues. Her competence earned her a promotion. She is now a manager of the company's branch at a new site.

But things are not working out at her new post. The nature of the work is new. There's lot of pressure and time constraints. Worse, it's a hostile work environment. Internal politics are active in her new office. The extra income cannot compensate for the aggravation.

Let me tell you about an army general.

A general's unit had marched seven miles forward. His unit came under fire from the enemy. He retreated to the higher ground that they had previously encamped. He told his soldiers, "It's okay to lose a battle in order to win a war." In that old place, he developed a new strategy to conquer the enemy.

Let's say that Emily's previous job was at level 100, and her new job is at 110. If she returns to the 100 level (back to her previous position), she is copying the strategy of the general.

What's more desirable and satisfactory, to succeed as a supervisor or to fail as a manager?

Of course succeeding is more appealing. It pays to be a successful supervisor.

Don't Treat Me Like a Servant

Bobby shouted, "I'm sick of people treating me like a servant. I worked harder than others. I did everything the supervisor asked me. Did I get the raise? No. Jeff, who didn't lift a finger, got it."

"You said that you frequently helped Jeff finish his work, right?" I asked.

"Yes. He would beg me to do his stuff while he took his girlfriend out," he confirmed.

"What did you tell him?" I delved further to see how he dealt with these requests.

He looked embarrassed before he said, "What could I say? I couldn't refuse. Everybody knows that I'm very helpful."

"Supervisors know how to delegate work. They know how to deal with people who are working *for* them. From your description of Jeff, I can say that he is supervisor material and you are worker material," I explained.

Bobby raised his voice and said, "What makes you say that?"

"The only thing you know is to carry out orders. A Spanish proverb says that if someone calls you a mule, ignore him. If many people call you a mule, buy a saddle for yourself. You are being treated like a servant, because under the guise of being helpful, you are *acting* like a servant," I explained further.

Ask yourself, "Instead of respecting me as a coworker, why are people treating me as their subordinate?"

Examine how you relate to people. Learn how to say 'no' to those who take advantage of you. The key is in your hand. Stop acting like a servant and people will not treat you like one.

About promotion, your issue is not hard work. You *are* a hard worker, but it must be coupled with leadership qualities and skills. Therefore, study leadership and learn how to become a leader. You can learn these skills at seminars, on the internet, or at workshops.

Chapter 25:
Why Choose to Carry an Unnecessary Load?

Making Their Problems Her Problems

Renee is socially conscientious.

When she reads a newspaper, she makes corrections when she finds misspellings, missing dates, or wrong places of events.

If she gets a letter, she writes back when she finds grammatical mistakes.

But her letter writing isn't the end of it. She cannot let it rest until she gets a response. If there's no response and they send her another letter bearing the same mistakes, she becomes very upset. She picks up the phone and expresses her annoyance about the department's inattention and disregard for improvement.

Renee does a lot of good, but most of her time and attention is spent on these things while her family remains neglected. She chose to invite trouble that was not hers in the first place. The problems of others became hers. This attitude made her unhappy.

Not all matadors in a bullfight are winners. Bulls *do* sometimes win.

Renee is like a spectator in a bullfight. She walks into the open field and challenges the bull. It charges at her.

Two things are possible for Renee: serious injury or death. The bullfighter gets paid, but Rene does not receive compensation because she had no business being there in the first place.

Stop overstepping your boundaries.

Stray Dogs and Cats

I have met people with an issue of multiple animals in their home. I have seen people living with thirty cats. Their original cats gave birth to more cats. They became locked in this situation because of the family's emotional attachment to animals. The unplanned adoptions caused financial strain. The cleanliness of the house became difficult to maintain. Worse, it was a source of marital conflict.

One spouse was kind to animals. He would pick up a stray cat, dog, or raccoon and bring it home. Once the animal was there, everybody would go gaga over it. In short, there was another unplanned addition to the family that was putting a drain on the family's time, energy, and budget.

If you see a louse, I'm sure you wouldn't pick it up. You wouldn't stick it onto your own head because you may end up having to shave off your hair. Though this example is extreme, it does point to the fact that you would never do it. Why, then, would you bring a stray animal into your home when your problems just keep getting worse?

Being kind to animals is not wrong, but don't impose every stray animal you find on your family. Set your priorities. Is animal welfare above family welfare?

There are animal shelters where stray animals can be deposited for emergency care until adoption. Call them and let them do their jobs.

Compulsive Helper

Let's say you're someone who loves to help. That's one of the reasons why your family, friends, and clientele love you.

Look closely at this scenario.

You are having a difficult time. In one of these stress-filled days, a relative, a friend, or a loved one came to you. He confided his pressures and stress, and asked whether you could help by taking over some of his financial and social load.

Once again, you accepted the burden, even though you were drowning in responsibilities to yourself and your profession. Your inability to say 'no' leads you toward physical, emotional, and financial breakdown.

There are only two choices available to you. One: decline. Let them carry the weight of their own problems for a change.

Two: say yes to the load until you are emotionally exhausted and financially paralyzed. You can choose to pull down the shutter and survive, or lie in the sewer and die. It is *always* your call.

Buying a Ferrari with No Money for Gas

Phil got married recently. They had a baby, and he worried about moving into a house that he can hardly afford.

When you buy a Ferrari, the cost of the monthly payment for such a vehicle will absorb all your income. You will be left with nothing to take care of the rest of the bills, including money for gasoline. How are you going to enjoy a nice car that won't run because it has no gas?

Buying a house you can't afford is like buying a Ferrari when you can't fill the gas tank.

The house will make you work two jobs to pay the mortgage. Besides being tired, you will start putting constraints on the family's food expenses and power usage. Instead of enjoying your home, it will become a source of stress for the family.

Don't bring stress into your life intentionally.

Selecting Photographs for Your Living Room

You have hundreds of photographs in your albums of different occasions with different people and at different ages. Some were candid and some were organized takes. You were neatly posed in some and wacky in others. You looked good in some and you wished it were not you in others. Some triggered happy memories and some sparked sad stories.

You wanted to select eight photos to frame. They would adorn your living room walls, so you went over them carefully.

In the same way, you recollect memories of events that happened in your childhood, teenage, and adult years.

What kind of mental photographs and videos do you recall and watch? Are they happy or unhappy ones? Are they worth celebrating or forgetting? Do they make you smile or cry?

You were choosy in selecting photos to decorate your house. Be *extra* choosy in selecting photos and videos to play in your head and adorn the walls of your heart. It's like saying, "I choose to only remember the good things."

Making Assumptions

A person scratched his nose, put his thumb on his belt, or straightened his collar. Ordinary actions, right?

My patient, David, would interpret it differently. "That person dislikes me," he would say to himself.

He made ugly interpretations of body movements, voice inflections, and facial expressions. Then he would withdraw from the person and miss opportunities to make friends.

Unless David admits that his assumptions are not doing him any good, he is going to remain super sensitive. A person that wallows alone in resentment is a ripe candidate for loneliness.

Speeding Ticket

Emma boasted about driving 85 miles an hour on the highway. Every time I told her to be careful, she would just wink at me and say, "I have a knack for getting away."

"Did a policeman stop you?" I asked.

"I know where the policemen are posted. I slow down before I reach those places," she laughingly answered.

In addition, she always parked her car without putting coins into the meter. She took risks with the parking attendant.

One day, she came to the office and was fuming. She got a $200 ticket for driving 85 miles an hour in a 50-mile zone. She kept cursing the police officer.

"I always over-speed 15 to 20 miles. Nobody runs after me. I had only driven five miles today, but this state trooper gave me a ticket," she said angrily.

She tried to be slick and said, "Officer, I'm late picking up my kids from school."

The officer replied, "Better late than never."

She was very upset. She totally dissociated herself from the part of her that took risks every day.

It can be painful to recognize that *you* are the cause of your own misery. When adverse things happen to you, don't forget to ask, "Am I responsible for bringing this on myself?"

Chapter 26:
Look Before You Leap!

Terms and Conditions

"I accepted the relationship with Ian and signed the prenuptial terms and conditions," said Yola, a New Jersey resident.

Do you accept it, fully knowing that some stipulations limit the relationship? Do you then live a life of resentment?

When you get a smartphone, you can download apps; some are free, some are paid. Paid or free, the apps come with terms and conditions. Some stipulations are okay, but the price you pay is often quite high. If you like it, you click 'yes.' If you don't, you click 'no.' In short, you have the final say.

You have your own needs and expectations, which may or may not fit the other person. The other person has a set of his own needs and expectations, which may or may not fit you. In the initial euphoria, both partners oftentimes forget that there are actually unexpressed terms and conditions lurking behind their passion. Some things are non-negotiable to some people like religion, a vegetarian diet, a carnivorous diet, or having children. These things must be discussed and settled between both parties before marriage.

When people come into your life, check what they're bringing to the table. It's like the terms and conditions of an app. Scrutinize it. Is the other person open to negotiation? Are you? Should you click yes or no?

If there's a problem in either of you, let it go and move on to other apps. Move on to another relationship, job, friendship, house, car, or other stuff that will not put heavy restrictions on you. Make choices that will not stifle your creativity, convictions, or freedom.

Marriage is a Package Deal

We were new in America and didn't know much about buying houses. As soon as we got the money for a down payment, we bought this nice house with a beautiful lawn. However, we soon discovered that, along with paying high taxes, there was gutter cleaning, lawn mowing, and other maintenance we had to keep up on.

The beautiful, huge house was exciting. However, its package of beauty and comfort came along with maintenance and expenses. We wondered whether we had made the right decision.

Buying a house is a major move. The expenses and responsibilities that the purchase entails should not be a surprise. Do research before closing the deal.

Marriage is also a package deal. You get married to the love of your life, then many things may follow.

Yes, your wife is gorgeous, but in your first month of marriage, you discover that her PMS turns her into Godzilla. Yes, your wife is thoughtful and a good cook, but she insists on having a cat and a dog. You have to choose between suffering her tantrums or suffering your asthma. Yes, your husband loves you, but your mother-in-law is an arrogant detective who snoops around the house and your lives.

Taking on Godzilla, asthma, or amateur spies are just a few things that a marriage might entail. There could be more.

Marriage is a major decision. The intricacies of married life shouldn't surprise you. Cover the essentials beforehand. In other words, research the basics of building a good marriage and responsible parenthood. Seek your family's input. Ask for wisdom from responsible married friends. Receive counsel from your church's priest or pastor.

After you have done all of that, the ins and outs can no longer shake you or take you by surprise.

Islamic Marriage

A state-appointed *Qadi* (a Muslim judge) officiates the Islamic *Nikah* ceremony and keeps a record of the marriage contract. The marriage vows include *mahr,* a mandatory payment in the form of money or possessions, paid by the groom in case of a divorce.

I call it the 'exit policy.'

People tie the knot in matrimony, just like any other people in other societies. The difference is that an exit policy has been drawn out at the wedding. There is no agreement unless the woman accepts the proposal of the man.

The *mahr* eliminates ugly haggling in case of a divorce.

Let's talk about the concept of an exit policy in some areas of life.

Do we think about an exit policy when we enter into a relationship or make friends? No, we don't, even when we start a business or buy a house.

What happens if a vacation plan fizzles out or a husband becomes violent? How are we going to handle things emotionally and financially?

Since an exit policy has never entered our minds, we leave ourselves open to emotional and financial surprises.

The exit policy in an Islamic marriage makes it easy on everybody in terms of financial issues. Thinking about an exit policy in relationships in our life decreases the pressure. We won't find ourselves in a tight position.

An exit policy is not pessimism. It's like growing a hedge of protection around you.

Lifeboats on a Big Ship

Big ships look invincible. They are made to endure and withstand adverse weather. They give the impression that they're going to last forever. But from time to time, they meet tragedies at sea due to mechanical trouble, fire, storms, or collision. In these cases, everybody scurries to grab a lifeboat.

Most passengers don't give a second thought to lifeboats when they're on a cruise. Most are not even interested in knowing where the lifeboats are located. But everybody practically throws themselves into those lifeboats when tragedy strikes.

How does this apply to relationships?

Losing one's identity is true for some women. As soon as she gets herself a boyfriend or a husband, she feels secure. It's like being on a big, sturdy ship. She becomes lost in his world – his desires, needs, dreams, family, friends, and earnings. She becomes neglectful and lazy in maintaining her own relationships with her girlfriends, loved ones, and relatives. She loses interest in continuing her hobbies, education, and profession. These are lifeboats and life vests, but she is leaving them on the shore.

Eventually, fear grips her.

"What will I do if the relationship goes sour and we get divorced? I'll be lost if the marriage sinks."

Therefore, though you go aboard a big ship, don't be negligent. Check where the lifeboats and life jackets are so you know where to reach them when you need them. The boat may not sink, but what if it does?

Chapter 27:
Holding Your Tongue

Is Your Filter Defective?

It was hot inside the house. I thought that the air conditioner might be broken, so I called a technician.

He examined it and said, "The filter is inadequate; change it." We changed the filter and the house became a cool place again.

Martina believed that she had to say whatever came into her head. Her brain was slow and her tongue was fast. Before she considered the full idea, her tongue popped out the words like hot popcorn. She blurted out uncensored words regardless of who her audience was: friends, parents, children, or her husband. She didn't think of the consequences. Her inner filter was defective, and this attitude created difficulties for her.

Do you feel that others argue with you? Is there always controversy around you?

It takes two to tango. Your filter may be defective. What have you said that put you in a problematic situation?

Get a new filter to calm your head. When you get a thought and a strong urge to say something, first ask, "What will result from this statement? Am I divulging something that's supposed to be secret, personal, or sensitive? When I bring this out, will it benefit me or the person hearing it?"

We can't run amok with our tongues. Filters are an essential part of peaceful living.

Take it to Your Grave

You entrusted a secret to somebody. If *you* didn't keep it to yourself, what made you think that the person you told it to would keep it? Your story may have gotten spread around town.

On the flipside, people have also entrusted their sensitive matters to you. "This is just between us. Please don't tell anyone else," they said and made you promise.

How many times have you revealed people's secrets to others, especially when your relationship with the person became strained or the person was no longer in your life for whatever reason?

"See? I'm the only one who was privy to it. I surprised you, didn't I?" You muttered proudly to yourself as you saw the astonished faces of your listeners.

Sure, there's a thrill in divulging things that you alone are privy to, but from that moment on, you're in the same category with the person that betrayed *your* secret. You have also become a 'traitor' to people who trusted you.

You don't want this label, right?

So, hold your tongue. Resist the temptation. Make a definite promise of carrying the skeletons of others to your grave with you.

What Kind of Gun Are You?

There are two types of guns.

One type is a revolver. You fire one shot by pulling the trigger. You can fire as many times as you want, but it can only be done one bullet at a time. Your aim is clear. You're like a police officer trained to shoot parts of the body that may cause injury but not death.

The other type is a high-powered machine gun. Hundreds of bullets come out with just one pull of the trigger, causing death and destruction.

How does this apply to people?

We may use our mouth like a single-bullet gun. We can fire words that are carefully thought out.

We may also use our tongue like a machine gun. We can fire words nonstop, not considering what we're hitting and how badly wounded the person might be, and disregarding the fact that the barrage of bullets could kill our relationship with the victim.

What kind of a gun are you? Are you the type who talks in a calculated manner, hitting your target? Are you like a machine gun that, once you open your mouth, ends up damaging your relationships beyond repair?

Explanations

I had an employee who became a nuisance. He didn't let go of his job as we had agreed. He threatened me with a lawsuit if I persisted.

I went to a lawyer.

"This is the one-page letter I have prepared. I enumerated the reasons why I had to release said employee," I said as I handed him the paper.

To my surprise, the lawyer scratched off all except two lines: *Your job will be terminated on August 1. Wishing you the best of luck.*

"The person was an 'at-will' employee. You could keep or fire him at will. You don't have to give him a reason," he explained.

I wrote a new letter. It contained the two lines the lawyer retained, but I added three lines of explanations. I sent it back to him for approval.

"The more explanations you give, the more trouble you are inviting. No explanations," he said on the phone.

In our relationships, we have the habit of giving long reasons for our actions. But the results are usually contrary to the understanding and peace that we expected. It wasn't the act per se that landed us in trouble, but the explanations we gave.

For example, you're supposed to attend the wedding anniversary party of a friend, but you emailed or texted, saying, "I can't make it. My brother is visiting. I hope you understand."

Your friend called and said, "Of course I mind. You're my good friend. This anniversary is only once a year. You meet your brother often."

You could have simply said, "I'm very sorry. I won't be able to come. Best wishes."

Next time, be a person of few words. Trouble is present in a multitude of explanations.

Chapter 28:
Share the Love

The Dog is Dead, Long Live the Dog!

He would tug at his leash and walk toward people. Gently wagging his tail, he would look up to make eye contact. When they pet him, he would move on.

That was Chui's demeanor, our sweetheart of a dog that easily won people's hearts. He was sweet and kind. When the children bothered him, he would run and hide under the bed and cry.

He developed congestive heart failure during the last days of his life. The local doctor could no longer treat him, so we took him to a specialized animal hospital 50 miles away. We traveled every day to visit him.

Chui died.

I was so affected. I swore never to get a dog again.

Two days after Chui's cremation, I was peacefully reading.

"Harish, please let me have this dog," my wife said, showing me the picture of a puppy on the internet that was being sold by a dog breeder in Oregon, thousands of miles from us.

What? I couldn't believe it!

"Please!" she pleaded, wearing a hungry beggar look to get my approval.

"Don't you remember the anguish that the family went through seeing Chui suffer? That's too much to go through again," I reasoned.

"Don't you remember the 14 years of wonderful companionship with Chui? Why are you focusing on the last days of his life?" she countered.

We kept repeating ourselves. I focused on our heartbreak; my wife stressed our happy years with Chui.

"I have had dogs since childhood. A couple of them had epilepsy. It was painful to see, but we always had the next dog."

My wife's attitude made me recognized this truth: people with abundant love are not burned by their sad experience. Love's overflow moves them forward to love again.

Accept Affection Like a Dog

Toofy, my dog, readily accepts any display of affection when anyone in my family caresses his fur, pats his head, or hugs him. He always shows his delight by wagging his tail. He comes running to meet me even if I forgot to feed or walk him. He wags his tail and receives whatever attention I give him.

Unlike Toofy, a great number of people aren't responsive to their loved ones. They brush off people's loving gestures when they're watching TV, reading a book, or tinkering with the computer. The common response is, "I'm busy right now. I'll talk to you later," or, "Not now."

Is the activity at hand more valuable than someone trying to connect with you in a loving manner?

A Lived-In House

I was driving down a street admiring the nice houses and their manicured landscapes. Each garden's top condition was obviously a product of good tending.

Then I saw a desolate house. It was an eyesore among that row of houses. The house's lawn, shrubs, and ornamental plants were dry and brown, a result of neglect. One matchstick would easily start a fire.

We are like a lived-in house surrounded by green, healthy plants when our life is full of people we love. We care and do things for them. It includes going to weddings, birthdays, or anniversary celebrations. We get a dress and accessories ready, prepare a suit with a nice tie, get a haircut, get a manicure, and buy comfortable shoes for dancing. These preparations are like beautifying and taking care of the lawn and plants. Our smiles, hugs, kisses, ardent greetings, and words of encouragement to the people we love are like the lush greenery of a lived-in house.

You can't give what you don't possess. A heart devoid of love doesn't care to do even small things for people close to him. He is alone most of the time. He is like a bare, abandoned house with withered plants all around.

Infatuation

I saw a 'For Sale' sign on a house located at the top of a hill. I saw the well-lit skyline of New York City. It was a grand view at night.

I fantasized sitting on the porch, looking at the magnificent view of New York, breathing in the marvel before my eyes, and saying with my loved ones, "Wow! How beautiful!"

I passed by the house a few times. I recognized that the path to it would be treacherous during winter. It was also on a busy road, which was unsafe for my grandchildren and our dog.

"Oh, the marvelous skyline!" This thought turned into an obsession. But as the days passed by, my eyes finally opened up to the property's weaknesses.

How does this work with human relationships?

In life, one aspect of a job, an opportunity, or a person we meet may take our breath away. If we make decisions based on that one aspect, we may be stuck with all the other flaws that we never bargained for.

Let your excitement simmer down before making decisions. Reason may replace infatuation.

Do you still feel the same after all considerations? Then it's no longer infatuation but love. Love may now decide. There should be no or few regrets in love.

Make decisions based on love, never on infatuation.

Chapter 29:
For Your Information

The Bladder

I awoke at 4:30 one morning and I was still sleepy. My eyes were closed, but I was conscious. I found myself worrying about something. I was tossing in my bed for twenty minutes. Finally, I opened my eyes. The pressure in my bladder became uncomfortable. I went to the bathroom.

When I returned to bed, the pressure in my mind was gone. The worry disappeared. I tried to recall what it was in my head that got me worrying, but I couldn't remember.

What happened?

When the bladder is full, there's pressure that causes a feedback loop to the brain that resembles anxiety and stress. If it happens during the daytime, you get irritable and will have less concentration. If it happens during the night, you will have dreams and worry. You won't be able to pinpoint the reason for your concern.

In reality, nothing is wrong. Your body is trying to continue its sleep, but since your bladder is full, it's waking you up so you can relieve yourself.

Watch your physiology. Keeping your bladder empty is not only good for your bladder's health but also for your mental health.

Can Marijuana Cause Schizophrenia?

Can marijuana cause schizophrenia?

There is no research that shows it can. The answer is no.

But if the person is already suffering from schizophrenia and introduces marijuana to his system, it can precipitate or worsen the illness.

The wind cannot create a fire. But if there is a small flame and the wind blows at it, the flame can grow into an uncontrollable fire and destroy your house.

Marijuana and the wind are the aggravating factors in these cases, but they are not the causative factor like the flame.

Two Kinds of Illnesses

There are two types of physical illness. One is biological in nature, like a brain tumor. We don't know what causes it; therefore, we cannot prevent it. Others are 'lifestyle' illnesses. A sedentary lifestyle with lack of exercise and excessive food intake may cause diabetes. The diseases caused by cigarette smoking, eating unhealthy foods, or being sedentary are preventable lifestyle diseases.

Psychiatric illnesses are also of two kinds. Some are biological in nature. We don't know what causes schizophrenia or bipolar disorder. Excessive consumption of alcohol, illegal drugs, a driven lifestyle, and domestic violence can lead to psychiatric illnesses like depression or post-traumatic stress disorder.

At present, we have no control over the development of biological diseases. We can only give them good medical attention. Exercise and diet can prevent the diseases caused by a person's lifestyle, like diabetes.

Watch your intake of chemical substances. Balance play with work in order to avoid burnout. Give and get emotional support when needed by developing a network of friends and family. Avoid extramarital affairs to prevent sexually transmitted diseases and a breakup of your marriage.

Watch your actions and habits. Don't create mental illness for yourself and your family.

The Explanation

I visited a village temple during my field training in medical school. It was the temple of the goddess *Devi Mata,* who was believed to have curative power. A village woman was in front of the image, shaking her head rhythmically to the beat of a drum. After ten minutes, she lay exhausted. Later, she got up and chatted with us.

"How are you feeling?" I asked with curiosity.

"I feel much better," she answered, combing her hair with her fingers.

"What ails you?" I pressed on.

"I have back problems. The temple *pujari* says that I have demonic effects on my back. Going into trance with the music will remove the evil spirits," she said, her eyes full of conviction as she looked straight at me.

"How long have you been doing this?" I prodded further.

"For some weeks, and I'm feeling better now," she answered.

I was doing my psychiatric residency training in India in the 60's and early 70's. Back then we would say, "What you have is a disease. There are pills for it."

Hearing the words 'disease' and 'pill' would calm the nerves of patients. As time passed, we started talking about neurotransmitters like serotonin and how it affects nerve transmission.

In the last forty years, I recognized that there is a fundamental need for man to know the name of his illness and to have an explanation for it. The explanation could either be due to evil spirits, bad humor, eating the wrong food, indigestion, anger of the gods, bad constellation, or the planets.

Many patients displayed fear and anxiety. Explanations that fit their social and cultural background reduced their anxiety about receiving treatment.

Hippocrates explained illnesses through humor. Ayurvedic practitioners treated with the cold and warm effects of food. African cultures revealed it through voodoo.

If this is a universal phenomenon, it's important never to miss explaining the cause of the symptoms, the future plan for treatment, and how it's going to be managed. Of course, these will change according to our medical knowledge, but the need of man to know the problem and what can be done to solve it will never change.

If you are a patient, you have the right to know. If you are a healthcare practitioner, it is your duty to explain.

Live Life by Probability

There are hundreds of possibilities, but there are only a few probabilities in each situation.

A possibility is what 'may' happen.

Take a hypothetical example.

A patient who enters my office has the following possibilities: he could enter the waiting room, grab some stuff from my secretary's desk, and throw it at the wall. He doesn't like me, so he beats me up. When he walks out of my office, he's mugged in the corridors. He takes the stairs and falls. When he's in his car, it blows up when he turns the key in the ignition. The chances of these possibilities occurring are highly unlikely. They *may* happen.

A probability is what *usually* happens.

The patient enters the waiting room. My secretary gives him a warm welcome. He finds the room comfortable. He sees my good points as a physician. He may or may not decide to stay with me. He is safe in the corridor and on the stairs. His car starts without blowing him up.

The patient comes to my office for the next five years without any of those possibilities coming true.

Think of the 'probable' and not the 'possible.' When you are in a new situation, assess and weigh the probabilities and plan accordingly. To live in fear because of the *possibilities* in your mind is such a waste of life.

Chapter 30:
Channel Your Energy Effectively

Best Use of the Gas Can

A gas can in your garage is a source of two kinds of power. One, you can ignite it. *Boom!* An explosion of flames can burn your house down. Two, you can pour it into the gas tank of your lawn mower. Your mower can run to help you keep a beautiful lawn.

You were upset, lost control, broke things, and slapped your spouse and children. Worse, you shot at the ceiling. Your jealousy was like igniting your gas can. Your anger is eating you up.

Is it because you live in a small apartment and other family members live in bigger houses? Do you feel sorry for yourself? Do you resent them?

Focus your jealousy toward a solution that will take care of your problem. Sulking, cursing, or breaking relationships with your family won't help.

Pour your gas into your lawn mower. Talk to your spouse. Combine your efforts to work your way toward earning more and saving more. Eventually, you can afford to build your dream house.

Learn how to use your gas can in fruitful channels that will enrich your life and the people around you.

Invest Wisely

An astute businessperson invests his money wisely. He selects ventures that bring the maximum amount of profits possible.

Some people are like this businessperson. They make the most out of their 24 hours. Some people are also like a gambler who wastes his time and energy on things that don't improve his situation, add value to his life, or help him grow as a person.

Phil had a bad childhood. His parents died in an accident, leaving him orphaned. His uncles and aunts brought him up in a joint-family household. He was the 'go-to' kid, doing all the house chores and running errands. However, he endured and finished his studies. He later established his own business and started a family.

Phil is wise when it comes to business, but he is a loser in terms of time and energy toward his emotional well-being. Why? Most of his time is spent 'digging in the dirt of the past,' as he termed it. He consistently sifts through the muck of his childhood. Then he gets very depressed.

At present, Phil has real assets: a wife, children, and a business. He is also a respected member of his community. These assets will flourish more when he gives his energy to nourishing the present rather than exhuming the dead past.

Why the Aggravation?

My nephew, Sanjeev, told me this story.

He and his friends were having a good time on the golf course. Then it happened. A friend missed a shot.

"&%#@!" The friend cursed. He got very upset. It took him a long time to overcome his aggravation, so Sanjeev had to say something.

"You are very lucky in life. You have a house, a wife, children, a good job, friends, and a dog. You're in great health, too. But you looked as if your whole world was tumbling down when you missed that shot.

"We play to get a breather from the day-to-day tension. Missing a golf shot? Go to the stock market for a good dose of aggravation. There, your emotions might be justified," Sanjeev said.

His friend simmered down after hearing Sanjeev. He was able to smile again.

We aggravate ourselves with trivial things. If you miss a golf shot, it has no serious consequences unless you're playing for a trophy and a million-dollar prize.

When playing any game with your family and friends, keep in mind that you're doing it primarily for fun. If you win, it's a bonus; if you lose, who cares?

Healing the Burn

A burn victim loses his skin. A doctor treats it by attaching artificially manufactured skin. It protects the flesh from infection and losing blood. The artificial skin comes off once the natural skin grows back.

Be nice, courteous, and affectionate to those who are angry. Your unexpected warm behavior is like an artificial skin graft to interpersonal burns. A sweet disposition and a welcoming attitude are also great healers.

Will the other person reciprocate?

It doesn't matter. Just do the skin grafting and stay focused. Even a hard rock cannot resist the constant hammering of warmth and care for long.

The Dry Erase Heart

We write on a piece of paper. When the space is full, we get another sheet of paper to do another round of writing.

We write on a dry erase board. When the space is full, we don't get another dry erase board. We simply erase and write again.

There are people whose hearts are like a piece of paper. They 'engrave' negative criticisms on their hearts. Their space is full, leaving no space for positive writings. On the other hand, there are people whose hearts are like a dry erase board. They note things down, use the information, evaluate the situation, and wipe their hearts clean. They're open to do another round of writing because they're never short of space.

Are you very sensitive to people's comments? Do their words stick to you?

If you're tired of being like a piece of paper, why not change your outlook?

Of course you can! Always declare, "I am a dry erase board. These things are fleeting. I'm wiping them off now."

Refuse to invest your emotional energies on negative words. Listen, assess, erase. Move on and make space for positive writings.

What kind of writing material is your heart?

I hope you can honestly say, "I am a dry erase board."

Do Not Discard; Find Another Use

A homeless man saw an abandoned car. He tried to start the engine, but discovered that it was no longer functional. He checked the rest of the car.

"Hm, the roof has no leaks; it can shield me from the rain or the heat of the sun."

"Hm, the seats are solid; I found a bed."

"Hm, the windows can be closed and opened; I have proper ventilation."

Generally, the car was good to live in, so he made a home of it.

When a man's priorities change, he finds some things useless and throws them away.

When an accident happens, a body part or two may be affected. It may be damaged. The non-functioning part is like the non-working engine of the car. The rest of the body is like the good and usable parts of the car.

You see, not all is lost when a certain part of a man's body is incapacitated. Oftentimes, the limitation is just confined to that area.

How about the many parts that are good and usable? Continue to put them to good use.

A Quarter in a Parking Meter

Which direction should I go?

Decisions, decisions, decisions.

We are faced with making decisions every day. Our decisions can either ease us or make us tense. They can either free us or bind us.

One simple example: should I put a quarter in the parking meter or not?

You know the consequences. A quarter in the parking meter means peace. You're free to go about your business for the day. To sidestep a quarter means getting a ticket or seeing your car towed away. You have to go to the proper agency to pay and get your car from the yard.

Such hassles! What a waste of time!

A little consistent quality time with your children or spouse is like putting a quarter in the parking meter. It can pay big dividends in the form of a peaceful family atmosphere. Disregarding this simple 'must' in your family life will spell difficulties, which will surface sooner or later.

Pearls Lost and to Be Found

In my quiet moments, this childhood event is among the few cherished ones that come to mind.

My grandmother used to sing a song early in the morning. It was a song about the mother of Krishna, waking up little Krishna in the morning. She would sing loudly. It would irritate us kids. We asked her not to sing early in the morning. Her answer was, "I'm trying to show my love and affection in waking you all up."

My father used to wake me up, too. He would make little movements on my lower lip and softly say, "Dee, dee, dee." Unfortunately, this child wanted to sleep a little longer, so the gesture of affection was received as an irritant. One day, I told my father that I didn't want him to do it. His surprise was obvious, but he stopped.

Every time those moments visit me, I wish I could go back in time and collect all those pearls of love.

I'm determined to give my own pearls of love to my two little grandchildren. It doesn't matter whether they receive them with irritation or appreciation. No one could deter me from showering these pearls on them. I don't want to curse myself for missing out on loving gestures.

Chapter 31:
Expectations: A Good Boost but a Bad Boss

Fewer Expectations, Less Burden

I left my house at seven o'clock in the morning to go to work. I saw my neighbor, Marcella, exiting her house, which is three houses away from mine.

We're in New Jersey; she works in New York. From our location, the train station can be reached by foot in ten minutes. By car, it can be reached within a minute.

I gave my horn a tap. Marcella smiled, rushed toward my car, opened the door, and sat down. We said warm hellos to each other. I asked about her daughters.

We reached the train station. She thanked me and got out. I drove on.

This was almost routine.

Sometimes she would be walking on the right side of the street ahead of me. I would stop, she would hop in. Sometimes she would be walking on the other side of the street. I would just drive on. I didn't want her to cross the street and put herself in danger.

On days we didn't see each other, she never asked me where I was. I never heard her complain that I didn't stop and pick her up some mornings. She would always leave her home at her regular time, with or without me. If I was there, good; if I wasn't, fine. No fuss.

She had no expectations. In short, no expectations, no unpleasant consequences. Fewer expectations, less burdens. I always look forward to giving her a ride.

Rocky was the opposite of Marcella.

"I'm calling you this early in the morning to make sure that you haven't found a golf partner yet," he would say right at the beginning of his phone call.

If I couldn't join him, he would ask, "Is something wrong?"

We shook hands at the club the next day. His grip was limp. He looked away. He didn't talk or smile at me.

"Rocky, you should make more friends," I told him one day. I was burdened by his dependency on me for companionship.

"You are my best friend. How could you say that? Am I boring?" The hurt in his voice was evident.

His sensitivity to rejection and his high expectations of me were a self-made trench that he was going to fall into. I finally avoided him.

Your best friend doesn't mean your only friend. Don't be dependent on one person, otherwise your expectations will make your loved one feel like a prisoner.

Fewer expectations, less burden.

When Success Becomes a Failure

'*Kaun Banega Crorepati*' is a national Indian TV contest. It is equivalent to 'Who Wants to be a Millionaire?' Out of thousands of applicants, the organizers select ten people for an episode. Simply put, being able to beat thousands of aspirants to get into the top ten is a 'big time' achievement indeed.

One contestant won ten thousand rupees and walked away with heavy steps. His frustration and sorrow was evident. This was the countenance of Syed Mustafa Hashmi, a winner in '*Kaun Banega Crorepati.*'

Syed had a brother who became a finalist in the previous game competition. The brother won a modest sum of money, but the people in their town called him a loser. Syed had decided to join the game to vindicate his brother. His goal was to win more. But as it happened, he won less than his brother. Syed wore a look of failure when he left the show.

Why was Syed, a winner, walking away like a loser?

Expectations. The expectation he had set for himself was higher than what he had actually accomplished, so his achievement was valueless to him. The higher the expectation, the heavier the letdown.

A person who sees his victory as defeat has a faulty attitude. He is like the student who considered himself a failure when he got an A in all his subjects except one in which he got a B. This is a problematic mindset.

Look at your attitude. Are you a person who beats yourself up at every success you achieve because you're behind another person or an imaginary target?

Chapter 32:
Worry and Guilt Waste Energy

Stop Praying the Rosary

The house was filled with our voices. We were all chatting, but my grandmother was oblivious to us. She was off in her own world.

When we asked her about something, she would ask in return, "What did you say?"

Some of us believed that she was going deaf, but one day we discovered that we were wrong. We found the culprit.

Do you know what it was?

A rosary!

A rosary was underneath her shawl. Her counting made her unaware of her surroundings.

The rosary beads worked the same way for Simon.

Simon was always immersed in his negative thoughts. He believed that people didn't like him, but his belief was baseless. He had a good job. He was not a parasite to others. He was physically fit and well-mannered.

When he was in a gathering, he was unaware of what was happening around him. He hardly heard the conversations of people in the room. You had to nudge him to make him come back to earth.

Simon was lost in counting the beads of a 'worry rosary.' The negative beads were made of self-depreciation, fear, and insecurity. These beads made him deaf and blind to opportunities of fun around him, just like Grandma.

Is there a worry rosary in your head? Are you lost in counting and recounting the negative beads?

Don't miss out on life. Redirect your focus on your surroundings and savor the pleasure of each moment that life brings.

Worry is a Habit, Not Your Nature

"Worrying is my nature," Vince said.

"Wrong. Worrying is *not* your nature; it's your habit," I said.

Our 'nature' is unchangeable. It's like the complexion of our skin: brown remains brown; black remains black. However, we *can* change our habits.

Let's say you're fond of Italian food.

I may ask, "Why don't you eat something else?"

When you answer, "Oh, it's my nature," that is an inaccurate response. The fact is, you can learn to enjoy different cuisines.

In the same way, if you're sick of worrying, you can always change it. Every time a, 'What if?' crosses your mind, you can immediately counter it with, "So what? I'm moving on and living."

Don't Wear a Fur Coat in Summer

Did you know that worrying about the future is like wearing a fur coat in summer to avoid the cold of winter? The fur coat's weight burdens you. It makes you hot and sweaty. It prevents you from enjoying the sun.

Why would you endure the heat and sweat? Put the fur coat away. Enjoy the sunshine and the beach during the summer.

Worry Buddies

A worrier confided his concerns to a fellow worrier. They began feeding off of each other's worries. They became a duo of worriers.

This is like holding two candles, each with a one-inch flame. Putting their flames together, they make a larger flame.

A combination of people who worry is not healthy. Therefore, cutting down your talk about each other's woes will be good. Better still, don't meet each other frequently.

But there is some good news!

If there can be a combination of worriers, there can also be a combination of happy people. They make each other feel easy, comfortable, and relaxed.

Who is your friend? Is he a worry buddy or a happy buddy?

Smoke and the Dirty Rag

"I'm worried about the future. Will my spouse and children be okay? Will my job and finances be okay? Will I stay healthy? Will my life end up in chaos? I'm confused. I don't know what to do."

The future is like smoke in a room. You can't pack it into a drum or tie it into a bundle. You can't define it. It even hinders your vision and brings tears to your eyes.

Don't fight the smoke with a sword of worry.

Focusing on the present is like fresh air that dispels the smoke. The problem in the present is burdensome, but you can describe, define, and put boundaries on it.

The present is like a dirty rag. You can see the extent of its dirt. It won't become a spotless piece of cloth, but you can wash it clean. It is visible, concrete, and doable.

Focus on the dirty rag of the present. No matter how soiled it is, you have the power to clean it, use it, or replace it. If you choose to clean and use it, you can relax until the next wash.

Worry is My Friend

Mark was worried about his eye problem. The doctor recommended an operation. Mark had the operation done after worrying about the possible outcome. The operation was successful.

His joy was short-lived. He feared that the same problem might recur!

"You were worried before. Now you're at it again," I said.

"Worry is like an old friend. I'm familiar with it. It stays with me all day when there's nobody to keep me company," he quipped.

When we have nobody to spend time with, we make due with friends who teach us bad attitudes and habits. They influence us to worry or become vengeful. They have a way of putting us down. They also make us feel sorry for ourselves. We don't let them go because 'something is better than nothing.'

Is worry your best buddy? Are you willing to spend the rest of your life with this gloomy companion?

Give yourself a chance at happiness and move on with a new friend: acceptance.

Jay Livingston and Ray Evans published a song in 1956. Below is part of the lyrics. You can listen to it on YouTube.

When I was just a little girl
I asked my mother, "What will I be?
Will I be pretty, will I be rich?"
Here's what she said to me
"Que sera, sera
Whatever will be, will be...."

Next time you catch yourself worrying, sing the song loudly. :)

Snakes in the Basket

You worry about situations that you haven't explored yet.

"What will my mate's attitude be toward me in the future? What will the future of my company be? Will our house construction be completed on time?"

Before the problem even exists, you have drowned yourself in worry.

This situation is similar to a basket full of snakes.

There was a basket in the corner of a man's house. He heard some hissing inside it. He suspected that snakes were in it.

It bothered him and his fear increased over time. He stayed away from the basket, but continued to look at it from afar.

One day, he decided to lift the basket's cover to be certain whether his suspicion was true. He resolved that if there were no snakes in there, he would stop thinking about them. If there *were* snakes, he would get an exterminator to take care of them.

Recognize the basket of snakes in your head. Instead of avoiding it, find out the positives and negatives as well as the status and extent of the problem.

Then take action. Another probability is that action may not be necessary.

Painless Blood-Sucking Leeches

Someone was stung by a bee. He felt the pain and ran to his medicine cabinet. He applied ointment, took anti-allergy drugs, and called the doctor. Though he suffered, it lasted for only a few hours because of the steps he took.

A leech is not painful. If a leech were stuck on the back of someone's leg, he may not even be aware of its presence unless someone called his attention to it. If the person wasn't alerted, he would get sick due to blood loss.

How does this apply to life?

There are two kinds of worries. One kind is obvious and painful. For example, your bank balance has dwindled or your lawn is drying up. The source of concern is apparent. You can start working on solutions. The other kind is vague. For example, there's a successful attorney. He is well-reputed in his field and has a bank balance that will last him a lifetime.

His long hours of work are taking their toll on him. His marriage is suffering. He wants to go on mini-vacations with his family, yet the idea of working less billable hours upsets him.

His colleagues wouldn't be bothered by his absence because his work and earnings would go to them. They also understand that it's due time that he attends to his family.

The lawyer's work-related worry is like a leech that's draining his psychological energy. He has to recognize his need to slow down.

Slowing down doesn't mean sacrificing the quality of his services. It simply means handling fewer cases. With his robust savings, he has the luxury to be choosy in handling cases.

What can pull the worry leech from his mind? A firm decision to slow down.

One More Lump on the Face

Amanda had back surgery, but she didn't get the results she expected. Her visits to her doctor didn't bring anything except frustration and anger. She was growing unhappy.

She had to recognize that what she was doing was like hitting her head repeatedly with her fist. She was consumed with heavy regret, and it was causing a throbbing lump to form on the side of her head. Her back pain continued.

Worrying about and regretting a past decision is like hitting your head with a fist. It just makes you suffer more pain without solving your original pain.

Stop. The act is useless. Don't add to your problem. Move on without additional black and blue marks.

Self-Doubt

Dwight was worried.

"Sometimes I have sexual thoughts about guys. In a public washroom, I glance to the side to look at their genitals," he said with embarrassment. "Am I gay?" he asked.

"If a good-looking man and woman agreed to have sex with you, who would you choose?" I asked.

"The woman."

"Why?"

"I like women as sex partners. I can't imagine myself having sex with a man."

"Well, there's the answer to your question. You're not gay."

A gay man prefers to have sex with a man even if a lovely woman is available. Having effeminate ways and the interest to look at male genitals don't make a male gay. A woman who prefers a man even if a pretty woman is available is heterosexual. Nothing else makes you lesbian or gay. If you have doubts and you have tortured yourself about it, stop.

You Can't Peel the Potatoes of the Past

In my book *Metaphors of Healing*, I said that worrying about things in the future is a waste of energy. It's like peeling potatoes that aren't in your hands. Unless you're holding one, you will never be able to peel it. (I have a short YouTube video about this metaphor.)

The same can be applied to dealing with past regrets. Mulling over lost opportunities and relationships is like potatoes that were spoiled and discarded a long time ago.

The past is done and gone. Buy new potatoes and peel them. Get on with new projects, new hobbies, new relationships, new friendships, and new jobs. You can peel them efficiently because you have learned and gained wisdom from your missteps and blunders in the past.

Unoccupied House

What happens to a house that has no occupants? It slowly disintegrates. Cobwebs will be its curtains, worms will be its visitors, and dust will be its decor.

An 'unoccupied' mind also deteriorates.

What should occupy someone's brain?

It should be occupied by questions and finding their answers; problems and finding their solutions; otherwise cobwebs, worms, and dust will be its happy residents.

What are cobwebs? The unnecessary worry about something because there's nothing else that occupies the mind.

The brain is used to solving problems. If you don't give it realistic problems, it's going to create its own absurd problems.

Creating your own problem means worrying about tomorrow and nonsensical stuff in your present.

Am I eating enough? Are people looking at me? Do I look good? Are people ignoring me? Do I smell bad?

Do you think that a laborer who is busy digging all day will be worried about the sweat coming out of his body? Nope, he doesn't have time to care. He works all day. Then he gets home in the evening, showers, eats his supper, and watches TV.

A person who sits in an air-conditioned place all day without work would constantly worry. Am I still good-looking? Do people like and accept me? Do people dislike and reject me? What will become of me tomorrow?

The laborer's mind is an occupied house. The idle person's mind is full of cobwebs.

Feeling Guilty?

Illnesses like paralysis, cancer, and Alzheimer's cause chronic disability. The patient requires an ever-present caregiver, like a daughter.

A family member caregiver usually has one of three possible responses to these chronic illnesses.

First: She loved her mom because her mom was a role model as a parent. She took charge of caregiving, but it drained her energy. She neglected her own health, including a life of her own. As time went on, she grew anxious. She was stressed. She developed chronic depression.

Second: The mother or father was abusive in the past. The adult child refused to participate in their care.

Third: This is the most common. The caregiver has inner conflict.

Example: The pregnancy test showed the child as having Down's syndrome. The doctor advised abortion. The husband agreed. The wife refused for religious reasons.

The baby was born, and every time a problem arose in connection with the handicapped child, the husband resorted to angry tirades.

The mother felt sorry for the child. She was frustrated with her situation. She was having doubts about the wisdom of her decision to go on with the pregnancy.

The child died eventually. The financial burden and the weight of day-to-day care were gone. The wife was free to resume the life she had prior to the child's birth, like working. But she struggled with guilt for 'feeling relieved.'

Understand that she was not rejoicing in the child's death, but the fact that she could now take care of her own needs and get on with life again. If she were a bad person, she wouldn't have spent years taking care of the child.

In your case, you could have been the daughter who abandoned her parents, but you didn't. A big score for you!

Guiltoma

Guiltoma? Let me explain what this is. It's not a regular term. I just made it up.

In medicine, we add the suffix '-oma' for a tumor on any tissue. For example, lymphoma is a tumor of the lymph; meningioma is a tumor of the meninges.

My homemade dictionary has the word guiltoma, a tumor of 'guilt.'

I instructed my barber to trim my thinning hair. He gave me a full haircut instead. I made no comment.

I made the same request the next time. The same thing happened: a lot of my precious hair fell to the ground. I made no comment.

The third time, I requested the same... and he did the same.

In controlled annoyance, I asked why he didn't follow my instructions. He shyly looked down at the ground.

"I feel guilty taking $25 from you just to do some trimming."

"But that's what I wanted."

"Trimming just takes a few minutes. I can't take $25 for that amount of time and easy work."

"But I'm happy to give you $25 for that 'easy' work."

"I feel very uncomfortable taking $25 for only trimming."

We went back and forth saying the same thing.

Notice what his guilt did to him:

(1) He totally dissociated himself from my expressed need.

(2) He forgot his first duty: service the customer's need.

(3) He was serving his guilt by fulfilling his own need, not mine.

Man's 'guiltoma' controls his words and actions that are out of sync with how he relates to people.

Let's take a mother's 'guiltoma' when her child doesn't drink milk or eat according to the amount she believes is enough.

According to a child's body, his intake should be a baby bottle, not a large glass of milk, which is equal to the weight of his leg. A hot dog is equal to the forearm of a child.

Now let's look at a parallel situation.

If I asked the mother to drink a quantity of milk equal to the size of her leg, how much milk would she be drinking? If I asked the mother to eat a hot dog equal to the size of her forearm, how much hot dog would she be eating?

A child's little stomach equals the size of his fist, but the mother is like the barber who was lost in placating his own 'guiltoma.'

"Finish your food," she insists.

The child vomits. The mother has another round of 'guiltoma' because the child now has an empty stomach. She's back to her 'feeding mission.'

Mothers, be attuned to your child's needs, not to your own. Listen to the child. If he wants less food, it will not harm him to eat less. If he wants more food, why not?

I Feel Guilty

"I feel guilty," Jean said, "because I'm not always physically well. I can't babysit my grandchild."

"Do you feel guilty about the bad weather?" I asked.

"No," she answered.

"Do you feel guilty when it rains?"

"No."

"Do you feel guilty when the atmosphere gets hot?"

"No."

"These are God-created conditions, right?"

"Yes."

"Then why should you feel guilty about *your* God-created illness? If it was up to you, you would be there today. Remind yourself: 'I love to babysit. When I'm well, I will do it again. Until then, no guilt.'"

Chapter 33:
Tread Carefully

A Pressure Cooker Needs Time to Cool Down

You were done cooking. You turned the flame off, but you didn't open the lid of the pressure cooker immediately. You left it alone.

Why?

You knew it wasn't safe to open it right away. If you did, the super-hot steam would scald you. So you let it cool down first.

Ruben was riled up. He was like a pressure cooker newly removed from the flame. Just like the good cook, you waited and stayed calm. You let Ruben simmer down. You kept your distance as you let the enormous amount of angry steam dissipate. You listened patiently in silence.

Ruben prodded you to respond, but you said, "I heard you. Go on, I'm listening." That was all you said.

His steam continued to blow strong, so you said, "Let me think about it, and I'll get back to you." More than that would have invited trouble.

Dropped Soda Bottle

There were two one-liter soda bottles on the kitchen counter. I opened one and served it to our guests.

When I opened the second one, my guests and I had quite a scare. The soda exploded all the way to the ceiling. Our clothing and the rest of the kitchen were sprinkled with the bottle's content.

My wife explained that while she was carrying the bottles to the house from the car, one bottle had fallen to the ground. After the fall, the bottle didn't look different from the other. Its cap was tight and it had no leak. My wife didn't think anything of it.

What happened was that it became a 'soda bomb.' The excess pressure was just waiting to be released.

Jean was a guest at my son's birthday party.

"Where's Dan?" I asked.

It was a routine question when you'd invited a couple and saw only one spouse. But to everyone's surprise, Jean blew up like the soda bottle.

"You are a male chauvinist pig! If you only wanted Dan, why did you invite me? You only care for Dan!" she said in a hard voice, then stomped out of the house.

Unbeknownst to me, they'd had a bad argument. Dan had walked out on her, saying that their marriage was over; yet she came to the party while Dan left for the local bar.

A disturbing development in our relationships like a fight or an argument can transform us into a soda bomb. We look normal on the outside, but a small trigger will make us explode.

The things Jean said didn't apply. Had I known that she was upset, I would have dealt with her cautiously. At least I wouldn't have asked about Dan.

Being sensitive to people's state of mind when they're going through a rough time is important in relationships. It comes with knowing your friends' and relatives' personal irritants and moods. I had totally missed out on Jean's mood. My focus was on the general state of the party that was going on at the time.

I had to clean the soda from the ceiling, the walls, the floor, and the counters. I called Jean the next day. I apologized for aggravating her.

She was calm. She apologized for losing her temper and taking it out on me.

If you know someone who is like a dropped soda bottle, watch out. If *you* are the dropped soda bottle, warn others of your emotional status.

The Appropriate Time

If you don't know this truth, try it.

Cook in a glass pan. When you're done, pick the pan up from the flame and put it directly in cold water in the sink.

Be prepared. The pan will crack. It can't tolerate the sudden change of temperature.

To avoid damage to the cookware, let the pan cool down before you put it in the wet sink.

How does this apply to relationships?

When somebody is boiling with anger, don't meet it head on.

"The situation is simple. Why are you blowing your top? There's no need for it." Words like these invite a head-on collision.

When the person is lost in his perception of the situation, he isn't receptive to your interpretation, so don't barge in. Whatever you say will work against you. Your words will be like cold water that cracks the person and elicits angry cries or yelling. Though you mean well, the result will not be favorable.

Keep your mouth zipped. Wait for the appropriate time to spray your cold water. Stand aside. Give the person some space to cool down.

Cut Off the Thorns

When you give a long-stemmed rose to your girlfriend, you don't hand it to her with the thorns still on it, do you? You shave off the thorns or wrap it before offering it to her.

How does this apply to praising someone?

"Honey, you're a good golfer. I enjoy playing with you, but you're a sore loser, and I hate that," a man said.

Being a 'good golfer' is like the flower; being a 'sore loser' is like the thorns on the stem.

Give praise when it is due, but don't give it along with criticism. If you do, the recipient transfers her focus from the praise to the criticism.

Separate the flower from the thorns like this:

"I want to give you feedback I consider negative. Are you open to hearing me out in the spirit of good faith? It will improve the way I feel toward you."

The woman may say, "Not at this time. I'm not in the mood to hear criticism."

You say, "Okay, I'll speak with you about it tomorrow. Have a good day."

If the person says, "Okay, sure. Go ahead, tell me."

You say, "When you lose, you curse and people around us stare at you. I'd like you to keep your voice down."

By keeping your comment on a behavioral level, you can cut off the thorns without destroying the flower. You have described her behavior without passing judgment or calling her a name. But if you combine the two, she may wonder what you meant by your criticism since you just gave her a compliment.

Don't Be Intrusive

We don't like people who stick their noses into our affairs. These people may be our parents, bosses, and friends; therefore, we can't simply say, "Go away!"

What about *your* behavior? Do you think you only give helpful suggestions?

Let's examine the difference between suggestion and intrusion. A suggestion given without being invited is an intrusion. Did the person *ask* you for advice?

If he didn't, bite your tongue and swallow your words. But if you're eager to share, say, "I have a suggestion to make. Are you open to it?"

If he says yes, give it.

When you see arched eyebrows or squinted eyes, don't push. When you repeat or push it, you become an intruder.

Don't Break the Egg

If you hold an egg by its top and bottom part and press hard, it's almost impossible to break it. If you press the egg on its sides, it breaks easily.

How does this apply to human relationships?

You have known Rita for an extended period. You have knowledge of her strengths and vulnerabilities. She has shared her family secrets with you. If you call her names and reveal her secrets to others to prove a point, you're pressing the egg on its sides. She will probably start crying or screaming nasty words. But if you press her 'lengthwise,' she won't lose her cool. Your discourse will be productive.

Ask yourself, "How can I deal with this person sensitively?"

It could mean more assertively or more gently, after meals or during a vacation, on a Saturday night or a Sunday morning when she's usually more relaxed.

If your goal is to break the egg, go ahead, make her break down. If you want to resolve issues and for her to remain logical, don't hurt her.

Be Prepared for Spillage

The Christmas party for fifty guests in our home was going well. All of a sudden, two voices soared above the sounds of merriment. Two of our guests were obviously in an argument. Some crying ensued. The party came to a standstill. For about twenty minutes, we were bound by heightened emotions.

It reminded me of a plumber's method in solving my bathroom problem.

The washbasin was clogged up. The plumber came and inspected the sink. He went back to his truck. He was carrying a bucket and a tarpaulin when he returned. He spread the tarpaulin under the sink. Next, he put the bucket under the sink. Then he loosened the screws slowly.

Water started to come in easy drops. He made another half rotation, and the drops came a little faster. He made one more turn, and the drops turned into a steady but gentle flow. He squatted on the floor to keep watch of the flow. Then he removed two screws. The water flowed in controlled pressure until it stopped.

He filled two buckets with muck. Then he tightened the loose screws. He opened the faucet to test whether the clog was solved.

Then he cleaned up. He emptied out the bucket into the toilet bowl and flushed. He put his tools into the bucket, picked up the tarpaulin, and brought them all out. He came back with a rag and wiped the sink dry. He looked around. Seeing that it was spick and span, he said goodbye and left.

I was surprised to see that the stagnant water would fill two buckets. If I were the one who did it, the full volume would have discharged all over the bathroom floor and ruined our little carpet.

That was what my friend at the party did. He said he was just trying to help the woman. He underestimated her reaction. He didn't anticipate the volume of anger and distress that had collected in her heart. He wasn't able to control their talk, so it spread to the whole Christmas party.

Sorting out an issue with anyone should include consideration for the right place and the right time. In this way, the spillage will not spoil anything that has nothing to do with the problem.

Wake Up *a la Carte*

Sleep is a sweet thing. Most of us are sensitive about how others wake us up.

My aunt asked me to rouse my cousin from sleep when I was just a kid. I called her name and shook her arm. She sat up angrily, slapped my face, and fell asleep again. It shocked me for a few seconds. Then I retaliated by beating her up with the might of an eighth-grader. She cried so hard that the family had to pacify her.

Kids were upset with our grandmother for singing religious songs early in the morning. She was surprised when we complained. She thought she was doing the loving act of waking us up as if we were Lord Krishna.

I touched her shoulder softly when my wife's alarm went off, but she didn't stir. She told me afterward that she preferred me to say her name.

Find out from your loved ones how they would like to you to wake them up. A gentle touch on their shoulder, a kiss on their forehead, or bending their big toe is enough for some. Others like a feather-like tickle on their heel, a gentle combing of their hair, or an aroma of coffee.

Do you want a great morning? Carry out the small request based on their instruction.

Post Script

An argument was getting heated. You wanted to avoid further escalation, so you walked away from it; however, this was misinterpreted.

"He left in a huff. Am I like a dog barking for nothing?" the other person fumed.

Don't just disappear like a bubble. Say something before you exit.

Gently say something like this:

"Let me think. We'll pick this up the next time we meet."

"Give me some time to think about it. I'll get back to you."

"I see your point of view. Let's discuss it next time."

You refused to be pulled into the argument. Good for you! But you also walked away from the heat, leaving behind some wise words to give you both time to cool down.

Call the Hotline

Trained firemen storm inside burning houses to rescue people who are trapped inside. They try to save as many lives as they can and take care of the fire without hurting themselves. They're equipped with fireproof garments, oxygen cylinders, and the knowledge and training they need to fight fires successfully.

Trained professionals like counselors, psychologists, and psychiatrists are like firemen. They're always prepared to snatch patients from the heat of their crisis without getting burned themselves, and to protect themselves by staying emotionally separate.

When your friends, loved ones, or relatives are in a rancid argument, it's like a burning house situation. Violence between family members or friends due to alcoholism or drug addiction is also a burning situation. You may be called to help put out the fire.

When a fire has just started and the flames are confined to a small area, it can be controlled by a quick presence-of-mind response. When the fire gets bigger, it's time to call the professionals.

Walking into 'hot' situations is inviting trouble. The emotions involved might singe you. Before stepping in, ask yourself, "Am I capable of taking care of this difficulty? Do I have the training and experience to deal with this situation?"

Helping friends and family in a small crisis is a great thing. When the problem is beyond your expertise, get help. Call crisis intervention, the emergency room of a hospital, Alcoholics Anonymous, Narcotics Anonymous, Gamblers Anonymous, or the Domestic Violence Hotline.

We live in a society where trained people are waiting for those calls. Jumping into the fire yourself and not taking advantage of these services is folly.

Watch Out

The husband and wife, girlfriend and boyfriend, or mother and daughter who are in a close relationship end up fighting about 'small differences.' In the case of married couples, they also complain that their spouse is nice to other people but irritated with them for trivial things.

One of the reasons could be closeness.

People in close relationships may say things in a way that could be interpreted as insensitive, nagging, or picky.

The relationship is very close, intimate, and continuous without a break. It's no surprise that misinterpretations happen and aggravate the other person.

The Depth of the River

The depth of the river depends on the volume of water that comes from the river's main supply. The waves on the water's surface are influenced by temporary factors like a gust of wind, a stone thrown into the water, or a boat traversing the river's surface. Simply put, the waves come and go; the river's depth is almost constant.

Friction inevitably happens even to the most loving people. Husbands and wives, parents and teenage or adult children, and close friends are vulnerable.

A conversation can turn into a sharp exchange of words that may lead people to utter statements like, "This is it. I'm never going to speak to you again!"

When you have a problem with a VIP in your life, enliven your thoughts with the good times you've had with that person. Think of things you have gone through over the years.

The difficulties happening in your relationship are only the superficial stirring of the winds and stones of life. Trust the depth of your relationship to weather the superficial waves. It will calm you down and stop you from making mistakes, like giving drastic ultimatums.

Toothpicks in the Sandwich

My wife prepared a sandwich for me. Before I was out the door, she said, "Oh, I almost forgot. I stuck two toothpicks in it so it stays together. Remove them before you take a bite."

My wife made sure that nothing would cause the sandwich to open up before I had the time to eat it. Nevertheless, if she had forgotten to warn me, I would have bitten into toothpicks.

There have been incidents where people did things for our benefit, but hurt us instead. They got rid of our old clothes, documents, or books that we valued. They got rid of a pest of a buddy whom we loved but were complaining about. Nevertheless, the 'favor' unsettled us.

"I was only trying to help. I didn't mean to hurt you," the person said.

Believe it!

But the pain was mutual. You were angry for your loss; the other person was angry for your thanklessness and your inability to see his intentions to help.

Intentions reside in the mind. When they are given hands and legs that act, they bring positive or adverse results.

The person that trigged the argument wanted to highlight his intention. The person reacting to the situation underlined his action. Intention and action have to be synchronous to produce the desired results. Once you know the difference, it will be easier to rectify the resulting chaos... or avoid it to begin with.

Chapter 34:
Stand Up for Yourself!

Speak Up, Please

My wife and I were avid watchers of Indian soap operas. This was what we saw on screen one evening:

The woman was verbally and physically abused. Amidst the onslaught of force, she continued to look at her aggressor with doleful eyes, as if her sad face would stop the beating.

It didn't happen. The attacker continued to curse and hit her.

While the scene was going on, I was yelling at the TV screen.

"Come on, tell him to stop it! Come on, speak up! Run out of the house! Go into the street and scream for help!"

If real-life victims were more vocal about how cruelly they are being treated, there could be hope for their case. Their situation may not instantly turn bright, but one thing is sure: changes happen when victims stand up to violence.

Are you a person who communicates your situation by looking at others with mournful eyes?

People are not mind readers. Your eyes will never serve as a crystal ball.

Stop tolerating abusive behavior. Scream your lungs out so that everyone knows what's being done to you. If not, the beatings will never stop. You will end up like a dog cowering in a corner after being kicked.

The Meaning and the Means

Mila was admitted to a psychiatric unit under my care. She overdosed on pills after her boyfriend had savagely beaten her up. She had bruises and broken ribs. She cried as she expressed how cruel her boyfriend was. The same domestic violence was the reason for her previous admissions.

I saw Mila hugging and kissing a man that same evening. I approached them.

"Doc, this is my boyfriend," she announced. She had her arms around him.

The man, who was amorous toward her, was obviously drunk.

I asked to see Mila in private.

"What are you doing? Why are you with your boyfriend?"

"Oh, Doc, he apologized. He was jealous. He said he loves me so much that he can't bear to see another man near me. He said, 'When I beat you up, it means you're all mine. My beating is a sign of my love for you,'" she explained.

Mila totally believed her boyfriend. She had set herself up for the next show of his love: another beating.

Both of them didn't understand the difference between the 'meaning' and the 'means.' The *meaning* of her boyfriend's beating was his 'love' for her. The *means* he was using to express his love were the beatings. She must realize that the *meaning* of love and the *means* by which the boyfriend expresses it are two separate areas of a relationship.

People make mistakes. They confuse the m*eaning* and the *means*. Even if the *meaning* is acceptable, the *means* may be unacceptable.

If the means by which your spouse conveys his love is destructive or violent, tell him to stop it. Say, "Please find another means that will make me happily feel your meaning."

Both of them should get a healthy dose of understanding; otherwise, the relationship will eventually lead to a tragic end.

When an Enemy Attacks

In the movies, we often see two scenarios when an enemy attacks a village.

One, the attacker ravishes the conquered and takes away property and slaves. The survivors shakily get to their feet and repair their houses. After a short period of peace, another attack happens. The victims kiss the ground again. They get back up and work on another round of repairs. We don't see them successfully warding off the aggression by themselves. The only time we see the attackers defeated is when a 'hero' steps in to help.

Two, the attackers are able to pull off only minor disturbances because the villagers have their defense strategy ready and functional. After getting a beating, the attackers decide not to return.

When a spouse troubles the relationship through cheating or physical violence, it's like an enemy attack. It damages the victim's self-esteem, emotions, and body.

Responses vary.

Some people are like those in scenario #1. They have fallen to the ground, stood up, and shakily recovered. They have not done anything else other than praying to a higher power to stop the abuse. It is a sad cycle. They never come out of it victorious.

Some people are like those in scenario #2. They have been fortifying themselves with education and employment and taking pains to improve their health and physical appearance. They have become more aware of domestic violence by joining a support group. They have discussed their problem with the local police and learned how to face the situation next time.

If the attack comes in the shape of, "I want a divorce," they would just smile and say, "Go ahead, make my day!" They know they can survive emotionally, financially, and socially.

If the attack comes as physical violence, they have their defense strategy ready. They have a voice or video recorder to document everything. They call the police from the bathroom.

They also have a plan of escape. They press charges to throw the abuser out of the house and out of their life.

Don't wait for a 'hero' to sweep you away from a damaging situation. Be a hero to yourself. Stand against threats to your financial, emotional, and physical well-being. Go for self-preservation.

Good Yesterday, Bad Today

Your car served you well for many years. It helped you go to different places. You named it 'Sweetie-pie.'

Sweetie-pie's brakes failed on the highway, causing a serious accident. Sweetie-pie sat in your driveway for three months with flat tires, a broken window, and seats full of dust. However, you were hesitant to get rid of the car.

"It's been with me for a long time," you said.

You called an auto mechanic. He shook his head throughout his inspection.

"It's going to be hard to fix. The condition of this machine is fit for the junkyard," he finally said.

How does this apply to human relationships?

Emily loved her husband, Bob. They had a great life together. But Bob changed over time. He became increasingly violent at home. He slapped her many times and his two sons were terrified of him. She remained quiet about the violence, but suggested that they get help.

Bob refused. "There's nothing wrong with me. Go and get *your* head fixed, and take your brats with you."

One day it happened. He beat up and injured one of his sons because of a broken glass. Emily called the police. Her husband was arrested and later released. An order of protection was granted by the court.

Her husband's fierce behavior didn't appear overnight. A pattern had slowly emerged. It was unmistakably a violent one, but she and the children dismissed it by saying, "He's my husband," and, "He's my father."

The good times were the big factor for her and her sons' reluctance to break free.

The car was old, defective, and fit for the junkyard. Until it was removed, the driver's life remained in danger.

Emily filed for divorce. She pushed through with the court proceedings to eject him from her life. She eventually realized that what was good yesterday is bad today.

Flush Him Away

Your ex-husband drowned you with unkind words, beat you up, threw you out of your home, and made you an emotional wreck. He was like excrement.

When you go to the bathroom, the most natural thing you do after using it is to flush, wash your hands, and leave.

If you're a hypochondriac, you linger in the bathroom. You ponder and stare at your excrement, gulp the foul air, and smell foul yourself. In other words, when you spend your energy thinking and talking about your ex-husband, you're like a hypochondriac who 'stinks' of him.

Yucky!

So don't think or talk about him. Flush him down the pit of memory lane. The fresh air will be beneficial to you and the people who love you.

Stop Pushing a Rusty Wheelbarrow

Linda is a 63-year-old widow. Her only son lives next door. He is unemployed and hooked on drugs. Fay, her daughter-in-law, is working on-call at a hospital.

Linda loved her newborn grandchild. She took care of the baby's needs. Soon after, the couple started to ransack her kitchen until she found herself tending to *their* needs. In addition, instead of breathing fresh air while lying on some sandy beach, she found herself listening to battle cries next door. The fighting frequently spilled over into her home. The thought of her grandchild prevented her from getting away from it all.

Linda was weary and depressed. She made many trips to her doctor because of a physical condition.

I said, "Are you aware that your lifestyle is not fit for a woman your age? You're like a rusty wheelbarrow. Though your wheels are squeaking and loose, you're still pushing it uphill. You *think* that your cargo is your grandchild when actually your cargo is your addicted son. Do you understand?"

Linda moved to Florida during the winter, leaving her son and his family to learn how to live an independent life.

Chapter 35:
You Can Do Better

Change Lanes and Move On

"Doc, I can't come to your office anymore. I had an accident on the highway. I'm okay, but I totaled my car," Steve phoned.

"Change lanes if traffic stops in your lane," I said.

It's the same on the highway of life. If a problem seems insurmountable, why persist? Find a novel way of maneuvering through it. Steve was on social security disability income. People who are receiving this benefit can get free passes for buses.

"Steve, don't wait for years for a car. Get a pass and ride the bus for free."

Familiar, Not Better

I rearranged the furniture in my office. The rearrangement was the first in twenty years. Since then, every patient who had seen the old setup expressed their appreciation for the new setup.

"The arrangement is lovely, spacious, and more convenient," they commented.

Why did I put up with the same setup for a long time? I asked myself, wondering why the change didn't occur to me sooner.

It's the same in life. We maintain the same habits, the same mindset in relating to others and in solving our problems.

Why?

Familiarity!

We are faithful to familiar ways. They bring a disadvantage to our life, but we still stick to them like a loyal dog to its master.

Why?

We have always traveled that easy, safe, and comfortable road. We have been surrounded with the same stuff all our life, so we put up with it for the longest time.

Dare to taste something new. Stop answering life's challenges with your comfortable ways. You have it in you! You can discover the best that is still out there.

Wade in new waters and experience the exhilaration. The result will make you say, "Ahhh! Why didn't I think of this before?"

Using the Wrong Key Longer Won't Open the Lock

Rex is overworked and underpaid. He has a music school that could close any day.

Two and a half years passed by. His business showed no improvement. The water was rising and getting close to his nose. He was ready to drown.

He maintained the same justifications:

"Some instructors are costly."

"There aren't enough students."

"The overhead is too much."

"My house expenses are too high."

"Why aren't you able to open the door to pull out the difficulties in your business? I think you're using the wrong key in the lock. Change your key. A locksmith can make you the proper key. Go to the SBA (Small Business Administration). It's a government agency that helps entrepreneurs succeed," I recommended.

He did go. He learned new ways to improve the appearance and content of his seven-year-old website. His business attracted new students. Money started flowing in.

Are there ongoing difficulties in your relationships, finances, or business? Perhaps you're holding the wrong key.

Reevaluate your situation. If no solution is in sight, call a locksmith like your accountant, lawyer, or friends, or go for counseling to find new keys.

Gray Hair in the Moustache

We had a friend who ate with gusto. His moustache looked like a paintbrush every time he drank from his strawberry milkshake.

He visited after a long absence. We noticed some gray hair in his moustache. However, gray hair or no gray hair, there was no difference in him – he still ate with enthusiasm!

Let's make believe that football was your favorite thing to watch on TV.

"I lost my job, so I'm no longer watching TV," you said.

"If having a gray moustache has nothing to do with eating, what has losing your job got to do with watching TV?"

One hardship in your life shouldn't keep you from doing the things that you like to do. You lost a job; you haven't lost your eyes. Continue your interests in other areas. They serve as 'breathers' that temporarily take your mind off of the pressure you're facing.

Bundle It

Put things into packets leads to efficiency.

Usually we break tasks into smaller ones and finish them quickly. We take large pieces of furniture, disassemble them, and store small pieces in small spaces. It has its benefits. On the other hand, the opposite also works. Putting small, assorted things into one bundle can help.

I have lots of small stuff: tweezers, a brush to clean my shaver, a mini plastic bottle to oil my shaver, a small hair comb, nail clippers, and dental floss. I take a clear plastic bag and put these little things in it. Whenever I want to use any of them, I just pick up the bag and find what I need. I have clarity of mind and action. I don't have to roam from the bathroom to the bedroom to rummage through stuff impatiently.

Break the big into smaller bits, or put little things into a bundle. Do whatever it takes for you win the battle.

Filter Your Thoughts

We clean water in the pool by using a filtration system. Water goes from a spout into the filter. The filter catches dirt and allows fresh water to pass through. Algae and fungi can't exist in a pool with a filtration system.

The human mind is also like a pool filled with many ideas: irrational, rational, positive, negative, depressing, happy, and many others. We have a mixture of conflicting thoughts.

Have you noticed that people thank you for your good advice, but when it comes to your own troubles, you're confused?

Why is this so?

Simple. When a person talks to you, you *hear* his woes. From your ears, they go to your brain's filter system that removes the irrational ideas you heard. Finally, rational thoughts come out of your mouth.

On the other hand, when you're thinking about your own problems, you are *not* using your brain filter. The conflict of the positives and the negatives just keep on whirling in your mind.

Go to a quiet place where you're free to say things aloud. Talk about the issues that are bothering you. You can also record your voice or write everything down. Listen to the tape or read what you've written. The spoken words pass through your ears into different brain channels. The irrational thoughts are filtered out, leaving you with a clear message to find a solution to.

Rubik's Cube or a Game of Golf

A Rubik's cube is a puzzle game. Once you solve the puzzle, the game ends. The only challenge left is to do it faster. It's a result-oriented game. In addition, there is only you and the cube. It's a lonely game.

The game of golf never ends. There is no perfect way of hitting the ball. When a player gets a trophy, it's the beginning of his quest for an improved game. Joy comes from being with friends, exchanging jokes, and the ambiance of the golf course.

204

New golf courses, new companions, and new coaches bring new challenges. It's a process-oriented game.

Some people treat life like a Rubik's cube. They maintain a view that if they're able to attain a goal (financial, professional, or social), they have 'arrived...' they have succeeded, and that's it!

Bob worked 16 hours a day. He had sacrificed the joys of being with his family. He came close to a divorce. He became a multimillionaire and retired at the age of 37. He was doing volunteer work and engaging in some hobbies to keep the emptiness at bay.

On the other hand, the balance of profession, friends, family, hobbies, charity, and self-growth gives life the feeling of a never-ending quest. After achieving one goal, there's more to explore. The person can continue life uninterrupted.

Do you want to treat life like a Rubik's cube or a game of golf? The choice is yours.

Encouragement

As I stood outside my mother-in-law's hospital room, I heard the nurse say, "You are strong. You're going to stand up because you are strong."

One time I also heard my son and daughter-in-law say to their three-year-old girl, "You're a big girl! You can do it, big girl!"

In reality, they were not strong or big. Were the nurse, my son, and my daughter-in-law being dishonest? Were my mother-in-law and granddaughter being lied to?

In the case of my mother-in-law, the nurse's encouragement would serve as confirmation of her will to live. Those words were like a cheerful pat on her back that said, "Being strong should be your goal because you can do it. I believe in you."

In the case of my granddaughter, calling her 'big girl' was like conditioning her to her reality someday.

It takes a lot of boldness to work against an actual position of weakness and say encouraging words. The words were not dishonest and no truth was distorted. The nurse and my children were stating facts that were yet unseen. In my granddaughter's case, it would surely come to pass. In my mother-in-law's case, it was highly probable, depending on her body's response to treatment.

Appreciate past achievements; encourage present efforts and future goals.

Chapter 36:
Life Lessons from Your Computer

Block the Pop-Ups

My creativity flows unhindered when I'm free from any distraction that would throw me off course, like the recollection of painful or embarrassing events.

Knowing how bad distractions are for productivity, I installed a pop-up blocker on my computer. It takes care of irrelevant notices that would suddenly burst onto my screen while I'm working.

"I'm absent-minded," we often hear people say.

It simply means that various thoughts are vying for the person's attention, making him 'absent' from the task at hand.

Do you want to be present and alert?

Observe this pop-up blocker regimen:

Stop what you're doing. List the 'pop-ups' that are churning in your head. Prioritize. Arrange things based on importance. Attend to and do away with those at the top of your list. Put off those at the bottom for the time being. You will discover that you can pick up from where you left off with a focused mind.

Are You a Blank Screen?

You set up your computer, but you forgot to turn the screen on. Nothing was visible on the monitor, even though the power was on. When you switched the screen on, the computer immediately responded to your input.

The computer can be likened to a person. Our brains are processors loaded with a personality and consciousness program. People talk to us and we respond to them with words, gestures, and actions.

If we lack response to the initiatives of others, we can be likened to a screen on the blink. People don't know what's going on in our thoughts, in the same way that we have no idea what's going on in the computer without a functioning screen. Fear has stopped you from communicating your preferences or sentiments, so others cannot understand you.

Screwed for Life

You're working on an important document on your computer. After spending many hours on it, you pressed the wrong button... delete.

No! All your hard work vanished.

You paled in anxiety. It's good that computers have trash bins that catch deleted files. You can still retrieve it from there.

The point I'm stressing is to exercise great caution when it comes to important matters in life. You can't afford to be careless.

In relationships, there's an exchange of a thousand words every day through chatting, gossiping, texting, and conversing; but there are certain words that are like a delete button. They can cause you a lot of problems if you don't weigh the pros and cons of using them.

For example, the phrase, "I do," is a bombshell. Use it with serious thought. If you use it in a flippant manner, you could be screwed for life.

Why suffer? Hold your 'I do' close to your heart. Cover all angles before you let go of it.

Delete Your Browser History

My computer was very slow and almost useless.

"I'll clean it," my secretary said.

She clicked a couple of buttons, went to 'history,' and there on the screen was the complete data of everything I had done and every site I had gone to in the past.

It was accumulated information that eventually became useless, yet it completely slowed down my computer.

She emptied the storage and the computer started to work well again, fast and reliable.

Some people have the habit of 'collecting' things that happened in their life. Whether it's a job, relationships, or business-related, they don't easily let it go. They keep on reviewing and mulling over their history. The more they remember, the more the thoughts gain strength and the more they take root in the mind.

It's like working on a new project and suddenly, the old work you had done months or a year ago keeps on popping up on the screen. You make mistakes every time the irrelevant data pops up because you're distracted. As a result, you become slow and 'absent-minded.'

When a person says that he is absent-minded, it actually means he's not giving the right level of focus to the thing at hand because something pointless and unrelated keeps popping into his mind.

Make a 180-degree turn when you're distracted. Be quick to clear your browser history.

The Computer is a Gentleman

Vera froze with fear. The thought of working on a computer scared her.

"I might press the wrong key and lose the document. I may lose my way," she confessed.

I assured her that a computer doesn't automatically delete things.

"It always asks the user, 'Are you sure you want to delete?' He is such a gentleman. The permission applies to stuff in your garbage bin, too. In other words, nothing is removed unless you say yes."

Mastering the GPS

"I'm anxious about getting lost in the computer pages," Sheila admitted.

I reminded her that she never had any problems driving to work, being so familiar with her car's GPS. She just has to press 'home' when she loses her way, and the GPS will guide her home.

"You can do the same on the computer. Confused? Lost? You can always click 'home.' It will bring you back to your home page."

When anxiety hits the next time you sit before your computer, say to yourself, "If I get lost, I'll let my GPS knowledge guide me. I can 'restart' anytime. I can find my way without a problem."

Chapter 37:
Dear Friends

Mix and Match Friends

You wanted some company on a lazy Sunday afternoon, so you called John and Jack.

"Come over, we'll have pizza together."

"Alright, I'm coming," said John.

"Do you want to see a Superman movie? It's showing in a theater nearby."

"Okay. See you near the ticket booth," said John.

Jack said, "Why don't we go to the Batman movie instead? We can go to the theater near my house. How about inviting Charles? What kind of pizza is it? Where are you getting it? Could we get Chinese food instead?"

John's reply went along with your desire. Jack's modified your plans.

If you want it simple and easy, call John. He's happy to be with you without questions or demands. On the other hand, you'll be out of breath negotiating with Jack. He changes your choices.

If you want to get out of the house and don't have a strong preference of your own, call Jack. He could spice things up. You might get bored with John, who is more likely to follow what you suggest.

Select the right friend for your mood.

Friends Are Like Fruit

Some fruits give people allergies. They make a person itchy and red and have difficulty breathing. If it's severe enough, he's taken to the hospital. The person vows not to eat that fruit again.

Some friends have bothersome habits and horrible language. Each time you meet them, their words never fail to turn your face red with embarrassment. You hope your paths don't cross again.

Some fruits are delicious. People eat as much as they like because these fruits don't create any difficulty for them.

There are friends whose company you enjoy so much that you spend long hours with them. Taking a walk, having dinner, going to fairs or movies, and other activities are very enjoyable. You can't get enough of them.

Some fruits don't taste as good when eaten alone. They're only tasty and good to eat when they're mixed with other fruits or baked into a pie. We call the mixture fruit salad.

There are friends you don't want to be alone with. You're okay to meet them at parties or in the presence of other people. You say hello, you have a small chat, and you move on so they can talk to other people.

Becoming aware of how you react to each friend is helpful. You can wisely plan how and where you meet them, and whom you are with when you meet them.

Share or Don't Share

The next time you go to a restaurant with a group of friends, observe them. You may notice two behaviors.

Behavior #1: He wants to taste what's on everybody's plate. He gets a little slice of meat, some veggies, a small piece of bread, a spoonful of spaghetti. He enjoys every morsel. He feels good having tasted them all. He also shares his plate with anyone who wants to try what he has. He's the type who doesn't want to miss anything good.

Behavior #2: He's happy with his order. He enjoys his food. He isn't stretching out to pick something from his friends' plates. When friends ask to taste some of his food, he allows them. However, he doesn't initiate the sharing.

He's the type who knows his preferences. He's content with what he knows. He has no appetite for experimentation or a journey to some strange land. Trying something new is not his cup of tea.

Don't worry about whether someone wants to share or not. Don't embrace one and push the other away. As long as you enjoy their company, what does it matter? Don't you also have your own quirks?

The Burden of Friendship

The racehorse has no load to carry, but it is trained to compete, to run, and to win. A donkey, on the other hand, carries a lot of weight every day. He is burdened with wood, cement, brick, and other cargo. If he slows down, he gets whipped.

Friends can also be likened to race horses and donkeys.

There are friends who run together like racehorses. They compete in chess, monopoly, or golf. Who has the right recipe to show to other wives? Their competition never threatens their friendship. Some win and some lose, but it's a happy ending for all involved. These friendly competitions don't carry any burden for anyone. It gives their group life happy moments.

There are friends that make others feel like donkeys. They burden them with unending demands, which they expect others to accommodate. When they make phone calls, they never bother to ask, "Are you busy? Is this a good time to chat?" or, "How are you feeling?"

What are you? Are you like a racehorse who runs with your friends, exchanging fun without putting pressure on your friendship? Or are you loading your constant need of company or money on your friends, making them feel burdened like a donkey?

Do you have a donkey kind of friend? Let him go. *Are* you a donkey type of friend? Shift into the attitude of a racehorse before your friends see you as someone they can use.

Two Kinds of Gardeners

There are two kinds of gardeners. There's a gardener who, when he moves to a new house, checks every plant and sapling in his new backyard. He keeps the ones that are to his liking. He uproots and throws away the rest. There's another gardener who, when he moves to a new house, doesn't discard any plants in the backyard. He makes separate beds for each type, including the unusual ones, like the cactus.

The first type runs his garden with a policy of exclusivity. He excludes plants that don't fit into the picture of how he likes his garden to be. The second type has a policy of inclusivity. He doesn't mind decorating his backyard with all available plants.

People are also like gardeners.

A person may maintain his relationships exclusively. He avoids people whose attitudes or habits are short of his standard. He scratches them out of his network. He will be crippled in situations where help is imperative because his list is narrow and limited. More and more, he will find himself alone.

Another person may regulate his relationships inclusively. When a person bothers him with an irritating habit or attitude, he doesn't throw him out of his life. He puts people in his environment in different flowerbeds. He deals with each one according to the person's uniqueness. He would have a wide choice of support when he needs it because his list is robust.

What kind of policy are you using in your interpersonal relationships?

Choose Friends Wisely

"I don't have friends. How do I make friends?" you asked.

The flowers in your yard appear in two ways.

One, they grow like dandelions. They just sprout, an 'accidental' ornament in your backyard. You were happy to see them brightening your yard with yellow flowers. However, you realized later that their leaves are full of thorns and they're killing the grass. You now wonder whether you should let them stay or not.

Two, they come by choice. You go to the market and select yellow and red roses. You make beds for them. Roses are thorny, but you know how to manage them. You keep them for years.

Friends come into your life in two ways.

Every now and then, you meet people by chance. A new neighbor smiled and said 'hello.' Then you bumped into him at the market. Then you chatted near your fence. You became friends. With time, you see his problematic attitude. You have to decide whether to remain close or move away. If you have an alcohol or drug problem, you don't want enablers next to you. You have to say goodbye.

There are people who adorn your life through your personal choice. You are into education, so you make friends with people in academia. You choose people you enjoy being with and who also enjoy you. You pick people who you can learn from and who are also big on learning from you.

Choose your friends wisely.

Chapter 38:
Are You Truly Independent?

Paralysis Due to Loss

I travel to my office, shop, buy groceries, visit New York, and visit friends in my car.

A repair shop towed my car one day after its transmission failed. I stayed home for four days.

"My car is still in the shop," I answered when friends invited me out.

A cousin of mine visited us from New York. He came by train.

"How do you function without a car?" I asked him.

"Why should I keep a cow and clean its dung when I can buy milk in a carton?" he said.

"What do you mean?"

"If I keep a car, I have to pay for insurance and parking. I have to worry about theft and friends leaving trash in it. I keep a schedule of the mass transit system. Rarely do I hail a cab and pay the fees."

His outlook made me realize my dependence on my car.

How does this apply to relationships?

We develop emotional dependence on one person, whether it's a friend, a relative, or a loved one. We focus on this relationship 100% and exclude others.

Having a car isn't harmful, but don't be paralyzed without it. Maintain an active network of friends and family. If you do, you won't be lost when you lose people close to you through death, illness, or dissension.

Practice Being Independent

My father insisted on sewing his own shirt buttons even when Mother said, "Let me stitch it for you."

"No, thank you," he would say.

"Dad, what is this about stitching buttons?" I asked as I watched him struggle with the thread and needle.

He said, "It's a sign of my independence from your mom. I have no problem with her doing everything in the house. But in case she's no longer able to do things for me, I'm never going to be helpless because I know how to do things myself."

True enough, when my mother was bedridden for an extended period, Father never fell apart. His wardrobe never missed a button. He never grew hungry, because he didn't have to wait for anyone to cook for him. He served us omelets.

They had a loving, beautiful marriage. He passed away in his late seventies. In all of his years, he remained an active man who didn't burden his loved ones. He fended for himself even when people were at his beck and call.

Is Your Spouse Like a Boat with a Hole?

Don and Debra met in college. He was in finance and she was in administration. Both were intelligent individuals.

When their first child came, they had mutually agreed for Debra to quit her job and for Don to be the bread-winner.

Debra became absorbed in motherhood and housekeeping. She no longer had intellectual exchanges with her husband. Her conversations centered on the children's school needs or their headache, fever, or stomach problems. To make things even worse, she neglected her physical appearance.

Don had an affair and wanted a divorce. Depression hit Debra. She attempted suicide by overdose. Their parents came into the picture: Don's behind him, Debra's behind her. They were a family divided.

Don decided not to leave Debra on some conditions:

She couldn't complain when he was late coming home. She couldn't ask his whereabouts. She couldn't demand to go out with him without their children.

Debra agreed to all conditions.

Don was like a boat on which Debra and their children were riding. Setting conditions for staying in the marriage was inherently defective. It was like putting paper patches in the boat's hole. The boat would sink sooner or later.

Debra had to learn to swim so that she could stay afloat when the boat went down.

What does learning to swim mean?

Get a job, earn money, and find meaningful hobbies; relate to her parents, siblings, and friends. *That* is learning to swim.

The re-emergence of the self-confident, intellectual, and physically becoming Debra would attract Don once again. Finding and wearing her original persona that was lost in lopsided house chores would decrease her dependence on Don.

If Don finally leaves, Debra's new lifestyle will be a durable life vest against the strong tides in a single mother's life.

Post-It or Superglue

A Post-it note easily sticks to where you want to put it. When you want to remove it, you just pull it off. It comes off easily without damaging itself or the surface to where it stuck. Its effect is neat. The paper remains whole.

Then there's superglue. When you touch it, it's hard to get off. You can free your fingers only after some struggle. Its effect is messy. Your skin is left red and sore.

What kind of relationship do you create with people? Is it like the Post-it that is comfortable, relaxed, and easily separable if necessary? Or is it like the superglue, so sticky that any threat of severance would cause damage to yourself and the other person involved?

A relationship where you are unreasonably dependent on each other can cause lots of pain. Be watchful. A warm, uncomplicated, straightforward, and struggle-free relationship is the best to maintain.

Chapter 39:
Habits Can Make or Break You

Watch Your Pedals

When you're driving a car, you travel by either increasing or decreasing your speed. You press the accelerator to go faster or the brake to slow down.

The human mind has two types of thoughts: accelerating and decelerating.

Accelerating thoughts are encouraging. "I started and finished 15% of the work. Wonderful! I can do more work tomorrow!"

Braking thoughts are discouraging. "I couldn't start properly. I haven't even finished 20%; I don't think I can make it. I always fail."

In other words, thoughts either make you move forward to success or retreat in defeat.

Some people don't realize that, though they are highly motivated in moving forward, they are pressing the brakes. Then they wonder why they're stuck.

Ask yourself, "Am I pressing the brake when what I want is to go fast? What habits are putting pressure on the brakes?"

Watch your brakes.

Get Rid of the Clutter

We attach ourselves to habits, things, and people. Our immersion in them blinds us to the problems caused by such attachment.

It's important to recognize that what was necessary for our existence in one season may lose its value in another season. For example, a baby could not do without a milk bottle. When he grows up, the feeding bottle becomes irrelevant.

How does this apply to our habits?

Jennifer's collection of scrapbooks grew over time. The cutout recipes littered the kitchen, living room, and bedroom. When family members told her that the dust and clutter was a nuisance, she got angry. Her hobby became the source of arguments.

"You're interfering with my hobby, but you don't mind eating the tasty stuff that I cook," she complained.

I asked her to bring her scrapbooks next time she comes in. Then I requested that she show me a recipe for Tandoori Chicken. She started searching for it while I searched on YouTube. Within a few seconds, I had a chef telling me how to cook Tandoori Chicken while she was still flipping through her scrapbooks. She was surprised to see how fast I found multiple variations of the recipe on YouTube.

That exercise made her realize that scrapbooks were obsolete in the digital age. What worked at one time may not be applicable in another time. In that sense, it would be practical and wise to detach ourselves from certain habits.

Compared to Others

Comparing yourself to others is a nasty habit. You compare your house with your neighbor's and your furniture with your friend's. You infer that the other person or thing is either superior or inferior to you.

The illogical nature of comparison is seen when we bring the scenario to a highway.

Let's make believe that there was a Nissan Versa in front of you. You felt elated; you were driving a Honda, which you thought of as superior. But a Mercedes sped by. Your rejoicing was short-lived. Then you saw a Hyundai at your back. You felt like you were on the mountain top again. But your superiority vanished when a Porsche whizzed by.

Then you saw a service vehicle full of company employees. You felt superior seeing people who didn't have cars. Then you felt small when you glimpsed an Audi behind you.

Then your ego zoomed up like a rocket upon seeing a busload of people.

I told you that comparing yourself with others is a nasty habit!

First, your emotions were like a seesaw—up, down, up, down, up, down—so that you were no longer enjoying your drive. Your focus was consumed by whether you were inferior or superior. Second, you couldn't have known whether the Porsche's driver was headed to a court hearing for smuggling and tax evasion, or the Mercedes' driver was headed to an MRI appointment to check the size of his brain tumor, or the Audi driver was headed to the police station to fetch his delinquent son.

It may be possible that one employee in the service truck was recently awarded 'Employee of the Year,' and going to receive a prize car superior to your Honda. It may be possible that one passenger in the bus is finishing his Ph.D. in math, and another passenger sings like an angel.

Material possessions and external appearances are not the accurate standard of evaluation of a person's worth. So, stop measuring yourself with these factors.

Once again, I tell you, constant comparison of yourself to others is a nasty habit.

High-Efficiency System

As we evolved into more developed human beings, nature decided that important functions should become automatic. Blinking, swallowing, breathing, coughing, and urinating—they all became automatic. They are controlled by the autonomic nervous system. They keep on going without our conscious control, leaving our mind, body, and emotions free to attend to other tasks.

As time went on, brushing teeth, taking a shower, and eating also became automatic. Most of us do these things without planning because we trained our body to do so.

One example: Brushing my teeth is automatic, but flossing my teeth is not. It involves searching for the floss, deciding whether I should floss today or tomorrow. I am exhausted, sleepy, weak, and I do not feel like flossing. If I were to decide on the high-efficiency system, I would start flossing every day precisely at the same time.

Members of Alcoholics Anonymous say, "If you do things ninety times, it becomes a habit; it becomes automatic." If you floss ninety times in a row, it becomes automatic and you don't have to think. It goes into your automated system.

Postponing, cancelling, and not doing things regularly is a high energy consumption system.

Develop habits to save energy; then stick to them. You will be moving on, leaving your mind and heart free to do more important things.

Non-Responders

You sent an SMS and an email. You tried to leave a message on your aunt's voicemail. Her voicemail, as always, was full. You got zero response. But she hugged and kissed you when you met.

You complained, saying, "You never wrote to me or called me back."

She dismissed it with a wave of her hand and said, "Oh, I don't check my emails."

"Your voice mailbox is always full," you said.

"I know, but I don't know how to fix it," she answered.

This is like seeing your friend sitting on a sofa. You called him; he didn't acknowledge you. You tapped his shoulder; he didn't turn around. This made you feel rejected. You thought, "Well, fine! Screw you, too!"

How do you feel about a non-responder?

I call this a bad habit. It has adverse effects on a person's personal, social, and business success.

I hired John's construction company for two months. I had many questions from day one. Thankfully, whenever I called John, I would hear, "How can I help you?"

I praised him one day. "John, you amaze me. I called you 24/7 and you were always available. How is that?"

224

"I'm an ordinary guy, but I have been very successful in my business because of one good habit: I make myself available and responsive. I always have my phone with me."

I called John one Sunday afternoon.

"If it's not an emergency, can I call you back on Monday? I'm with my family on the beach," he said.

He was receptive to the inputs coming his way, and he was active in giving outputs. Wow!

Responses don't have to be long. A few words are enough. It may take only seconds, so non-responders have no excuse to be silent.

When non-response happens once or twice, you can brush it off as part of life. However, when it's consistent, stop wasting your time on those people.

Are you a non-responder or are you a victim of a non-responder?

The 'Later' Pile

You hate clutter, so you segregate unread mail, journals, and cards into a *later pile*. "I'll reply to them later," you promise yourself.

After five months, the *later pile* grew into a foot-tall pillar. Stuff started falling off the desk. You decided to put it into a large shopping bag. Then you set it aside next to your desk as a *later bag*.

Days passed. Another *later pile* took over the spot vacated by your first *later pile*. The pile ballooned after five months. You placed a second *later bag* beside your worktable.

The *later bags* overwhelm you. You recognize your hesitation to attend to the new mound of *later bags*, but you have persisted in your habit.

After multiple *later bags* have accumulated, you finally decided not to attend to it at all. You ordered your assistant to shred the paperwork and heaved a sigh of relief.

"I won't be taking care of it," is what you were actually saying every time you put papers on the *later pile*.

225

Recognize your tendency toward self-deception. Stop accumulating *later piles* and *later bags*. Throw things away immediately rather than piling them on your desk first. Keeping a *later pile* is like storing garbage on your desk for five months before discarding it.

Unlearn When Appropriate

My vision became blurred. My ophthalmologist told me that I had a cataract.

All my life the lenses in my eyes were transparent and aided my vision. But with age, they became a source of problems. A surgeon operated to take out those cloudy lenses and correct my vision.

Change comes in many shapes and forms. Coping with changes can be facilitated by openness.

Let's say that a boy grew up in a crime-infested area. Keeping a knife was reasonable and commonplace there. It meant survival.

He went to college and found a white-collar job. However, he continued to take out his knife at minor triggers or provocations. It created problems in his workplace.

He had to make a choice. He had to unlearn his aggressive habits if he wanted to keep his job.

What protected and helped you in one situation can harm and pull you back in the next situation. Learning and unlearning take a determined effort. Both involve insight, will, and self-discipline.

Irritating Habits

Most of us have annoying habits. A bad habit becomes the seed of argument.

A promising evening with friends didn't start well. Your husband came home late, though he knew that both of you had to attend this dinner. The culprit: your husband's habit of coming home late.

There is a way to weaken and knock out a bad habit without arguments.

Make 3x5-inch cards with different dollar amounts written on each card. It may be $5, $10, or $15. Mutually agree that your husband will carry these cards, and every time he arrives late, you say, "Give me your card."

The first two cards may be free. The cards that follow after will cost money. The amount on every card is progressive. Any day he comes home late, he has to give up a card with a higher value.

The cards in his pocket will be therapeutic. They're constant reminders of the agreement.

When he's late, instead of saying things that he may label as nagging, just ask for the card.

If he doesn't give you a card, it doesn't matter. You've done your part. If he gives you a card, collect it. After a month, cash in the cards.

It's not about money; it's about reminding your husband of his bad habit.

You may also use this method to arrest habits of yelling, drinking excessively, or calling you names in front of others. Both of you have to agree that he needs to cut down or stop any rough conduct.

Ask him, "What annoys you about me?"

Make similar cards. Use the same method and stop your arguments.

Nose and Ears

Cleaning our ears and nose is routine stuff, but it should be done with care. Sticking sharp objects into our ears could damage our eardrums. We could also spread infection when we're careless about hygiene after cleaning our nose and ears.

How many hours should you watch TV every day? How many vacations should you take each year? How frequent should your lunch or dinner dates with friends be? How many days a week should be assigned as 'exercise' days?

Taking these things for granted is like neglecting your ears and nose. This may create stress and complications. Engaging in these routine activities properly will improve your emotional functioning. When done regularly, they enhance life.

Changing the Destination

I have been passing through my town 200 days a year for the last thirty years. Every now and then, I find the street blocked by road signs: 'Road Closed,' or, 'Street Fair.' So I take a detour to my office.

Recently, on my way to a hardware store, I saw the same signs. I changed my mind as I waited for the car in front of me to move. I parked my car, took a deep breath, and headed toward the street fair.

I saw colorful stalls selling glazed popcorn, funnel cakes, lamb kebabs, seekh kebabs, chicken tikka wraps, Greek souvlaki, and Italian pizzas. There were stamp dealers, coin dealers, mask designers, and antique booksellers. I found interesting items that were far different from what we find in department stores. I walked around with Chicken Teriyaki on a stick that day.

The festive atmosphere was exhilarating. I was glad that I didn't whiz by that place.

Most of us stick steadfastly to our daily routine. There's nothing wrong with that. However, looking to our left or right every now and then will give us a chance of discovery. Who knows? It may prove to be a healthy detour.

The same is true in our relationships. We're lost in routine relationships with our professional and business friends. It may close the door to other opportunities of enriching your life. Try stopping and parking your car to explore the street fair of life. Meet new people, try new hobbies, or join dance classes or a wine tasting group.

You will never come across remarkable experiences unless you deviate occasionally. Stray awhile.

A Hobby Out of Sync

Food is essential for life, but eating more food than necessary is going to give you a disease.

Keeping a hobby is healthy. It's a delightful break from the stress of life. But when you use the family budget intended for something else or lie to your partner to cover up your extra purchases, it's like eating too much food. It's going to harm your relationship.

Luke is fond of tools. His basement is full of toolboxes.

He went to a flea market one day and was attracted to a toolbox that contained lots of tools. His mind kept saying that it would be an unnecessary purchase because there was already a lot of duplication in his collection, but he bought it just the same.

He was ecstatic with the addition, but he became uneasy with guilt. He hid the purchase from his wife for a month. Finally, he told her and it created tension between them.

When you're going out of your way to support your hobby or pastime, ask yourself, "Is it worth being out of sync with the other aspects of my life?" Then make a decision.

Chapter 40:
Thanks: A Big Little Word

Supposed To

I was sitting at the dining table watching Martina cook dinner. My friend, Philip, walked into the kitchen.

"Here's my paycheck," he said, addressing Martina. He put the check on the kitchen counter. Martina kept cooking and never said a word.

Philip and I chatted for a while.

Dinnertime came. Martina served spaghetti and sausages. All of us took big helpings.

I'd noticed something throughout the evening.

Later, I asked Philip, "Martina worked for two hours preparing food. How is it that no one in your family said 'thank you' to her?"

Philip was obviously surprised by my question.

"Why should I? She's supposed to. We ate the food, didn't we?" he asked me in return.

A little later, I asked Martina, "When Philip brought his paycheck, you just kept on cooking without saying thanks. You didn't even glance at him."

Like Philip, she was surprised.

"Why should I? He's supposed to. It's his obligation, isn't it?" she asked.

The couple got out of the habit of thanking each other. The idea of 'supposed to' stopped them from feeding each other's need for recognition, affirmation, and gratitude. It killed one of the key ingredients in building a strong relationship. Eventually, this neglect would catch up with them.

There are so many reasons to give thanks. The fact that you still have your tongue and the strength to say 'thanks' is reason enough.

Don't assume people are just 'supposed to' do what they do. Show your gratitude to help them feel appreciated and not taken for granted.

How to Say Thanks

You passed by someone and smelled the faint aroma of her perfume. You hugged somebody else and got a strong whiff of her perfume.

Compare the light and the heavy scents of fragrance.

Most of us would strain ourselves to smell the faint aroma, and most of us would hold our next breath to avoid gulping another smell of strong perfume.

Someone told me, "Spray a little perfume in the air ahead of you and then pass through that area. Microscopic droplets floating in the air will touch you gently. It's the best way to put on perfume. It leaves a gentle scent on your clothes."

How does this perfume metaphor help us?

Appreciation of others by saying 'thank you' or giving a gift is like wearing perfume. Do it in a subtle manner and the receiver will appreciate your sincere words or gifts. Do it in a harsh manner and your overdone words or gifts may appear to be a bribe.

It's a good thing to thank people, but be subtle like a soft whiff of perfume—perceivable, yet not overpowering.

Chapter 41:
Grow Up Already!

Symbolic Logic

In Philosophy, there's something called 'symbolic logic.'

It says: If Jack does X, he will get Y. If he does not do X, he will not get Y.

This seems to make sense. But you know what? It's false.

For example: If I work as a laborer, I will earn money. If I do not work as a laborer, I will not earn money.

Of course, this isn't true. There are other jobs that I can do to earn money.

Another example: I am married, so I am happy. If I am not married, I am not happy.

Of course, this isn't true, either. A lot of single and divorced people are happy.

Children believe in symbolic logic, but this kind of logic becomes weak as people mature. Generally speaking, as a person matures, he becomes wiser. As he becomes wiser, he learns different ways of doing things.

"I was interviewed and I didn't get the job. I'm not going to interviews anymore."

"I asked two girls out. They said no, so I'm not going to ask anymore."

Watch where your thoughts are going. Ask, "Am I using symbolic logic?"

If you are, don't you think it's time for you to become wiser?

A Grown Up

"I'm hesitant to charge for my services. I feel guilty when I do. I feel despicable. On the other hand, I feel taken advantage of when I give services for free," said a patient.

233

A child doesn't understand money, but he gets things because he is loved.

He becomes a little boy. Money is introduced into his consciousness. He learns to ask for and use it to acquire toys. The source of his money comes from people who love him and hand it to him for free.

In adulthood, he learns different skills needed by society. He charges people for services because it's his livelihood. As he grows older, he's able to negotiate better prices.

A little boy. A grown up.

There is a big difference.

The little boy gets money for free. An adult gets money due to his skills and services.

What are you: a little boy or an adult?

The Difference Between a Child and a Man

Matthew was the youngest child in the family. He was very dependent on his mother, who did everything for him.

As an adult, he joined his parents' business, but he remained under his mother's care. Then his parents died.

He started to connect with women. Unfortunately, his relationships with them were all short-lived.

Why?

He expected the woman to treat him like his mother did. It meant taking care of his every need and loving him like a child.

While watching TV, he had to have his head on his girlfriend's lap. He didn't care whether she was exhausted or not. He never heard his mother complain, so when his girlfriend did, he felt rejected.

A child sucks milk from his mother's breast. That's all he does, and solely for his own satisfaction. An adult learns to drink different kinds of milk in different ways, like from a glass or a cup.

A mother, a girlfriend, and a wife are not only different in spelling, but also distinct in their duties toward a son, a boyfriend, and a husband. They serve milk in ways that are completely different from each other.

A baby is unable to spot major differences. Every breast is his mother's breast. On the other hand, an adult is weaned from his mother's milk. He opens himself up to drinking another type of milk from a glass or a cup.

If you are a man, start picking up new ways of behavior and attitude in dealing with a girlfriend or a wife. Don't make your girlfriend feel like she's adopting a child.

40-Year-Old Little Girl

Two adult sisters got together. They reminisced about their childhood. One sister suddenly remembered a specific incident when they were seven years old.

"You snatched my pink bucket. You threw it six feet from me. The contents spilled out. I cried and you were laughing while running away. I was so hurt."

The conversation suddenly took an unexpected turn. The atmosphere went bad.

"You continue to treat me the same today."

She began to weave things in the present together with recollections of the past.

Normally, an adult would be roaring with laughter when memories of childhood impishness surface, but this person had regressed into the mindset of a seven-year-old. She sent herself thirty years back. She treated her sister's past deed with the anger of a forty-year-old. It was as if the culprit was an adult who smashed her computer on a rock.

This could happen between two adult siblings, cousins, or even friends. Don't bring today's adult judgment thirty years into the past, and don't bring past childish emotions into the present.

Chapter 42:
The Weight of Eating

Non-Food Celebrations

A non-food celebration is rewarding yourself with a non-food activity or item. It could be a CD, a new book, or going to a movie. If you are a coin collector, a coin. If you collect wines, a bottle of wine. If you are a golfer, a game of golf. You can take those receipts and put them in an envelope labeled, 'Money that I did not eat.'

Think of a $10 bill in your pocket. You can do many things with it. You can put it in your mouth and chew it. You can then spit it out or swallow it. Little harm is done by swallowing the $10. It has roughage and micro amounts of chemicals. Buying extra food is the worst thing that you can do with it if you're overweight.

When the number on the scale is high, stop wondering and cursing. That doesn't produce weight loss. Instead, ask yourself, "What did I do to gain weight? How can I rectify my bad habits that led to weight gain?"

Frustration Without Action

"I've gained weight. Oh, my God! Oh, my God! I can't believe it! I've been so careful. How could this happen? I'm sick of it. I'm doing everything possible, but I can't even lose a pound. This is impossible. Damn it!"

These were often the reactions of people when they registered 157 pounds instead of 147 pounds.

They didn't exclaim, "It's because I ate more," or, "I didn't exercise," or, "I ate food with high calories." They were so consumed by the figure on the scale. They cursed their weight and said, "The scale is defective!"

After fussing for a few minutes, that was all there was to it.

When you don't like the numbers on the scale, there are simple questions you can focus your attention on:

"What did I do to increase my weight? To bring my weight down, what changes should I make in my lifestyle?"

When you've determined that celebrating is the culprit, the next questions would be, "How am I going to spend today and tomorrow to bring my weight down?"

Take action without frustration.

Chapter 43:
Goal-Oriented Actions

A Tea Kettle Doesn't Produce Rain

A person facing a problem agitates his mind with anxiety, worry, fear, resentment, and helplessness. He tells everyone about his worries, but he doesn't translate his emotions into actions.

He's like a tea kettle making noise. The steam exits, but its extent is only a whistle; it's a very small-scale result.

Another scenario. The second person recognizes his problem. He changes his situation by taking action. He talks to people like his accountants, lawyers, and employers, or finds a new job.

He is like the sun. His rays fall to the ocean and produce steam, and the clouds turn it into rain.

The kettle's sound is only useful to inform us that water is ready for tea or coffee, but the sun makes the rain fall.

Ask yourself, "Why am I worrying? Am I taking problem-solving actions or am I only crying for help? Am I the sun that produces life-giving rain, or am I behaving like a noisy tea kettle, hoping that everyone else will solve my problems?"

Without concrete plans and actions, you will keep whistling forever.

Raising the Foot

Mona couldn't lift her leg more than six inches when she got injured. She had to use the backyard to enter her home.

After 15 days, I told her to try using her front steps. She refused at first, but her husband was able to convince her. She was pleased to discover that she could lift her foot seven inches without any problem.

When a person has physical and medical issues, his ability to do things goes downhill. He becomes so resigned to his physical constraints that as time passes by, his mind tells him that it's a permanent condition. He no longer takes the initiative to find out whether improvement is in store for him.

Nature has its own surprises for you. According to your doctor's advice, every now and then lift an arm, walk a few slow steps, or get up from the bed alone.

You've done it before; you may be able to do it again. Just try.

Housefly or Honeybee

I often receive emails and phone calls that say, "I've been busy with little things. Time just flies."

The housefly moves from one piece of trash to another. Every time it moves, it spreads germs. On the other hand, the honeybee snubs dirt and garbage. It goes to flowers, collects honey, and deposits it into a beehive. Over a period, it helps to gather enough honey for its kingdom's survival.

In three words, write down things you do every 15 minutes. Don't be critical. Just write it down.

At the end of the day, look at it.

Are you spending your day as a housefly, too busy with small and trivial things so time just flies? Or are you a honeybee with goal-directed activities like finishing important tasks?

If you're a housefly and you don't like it, nobody can stop you from transforming your daily habits into those of a honeybee.

Life is Passing By

Life is passing by fast, and life will pass you by if you dream, sit, and wait.

A dream is a goal. When you have a goal, you need to develop a plan and the skill set to attain it. Your goal needs your active participation.

Take charge. Earn money. Deal with people well. Take care of your significant relationships. Pay attention to your grooming and hygiene. Get involved in enriching hobbies. Be helpful to people you care about. Then life won't pass you by.

The Golden Rope

A man stood next to a well with a bucket. He saw water, but he couldn't reach it because it was thirty feet deep. He remained thirsty.

What was lacking?

No-brainer: a rope, of course.

He looked for and found a rope. He tied it to the bucket and got water.

Why am I talking about a bucket, a rope, and a well?

The bucket is man's intelligence. The well is all the educational institutions and sources of knowledge including the internet. However, they're not enough. The well water is unreachable with a bucket without a rope.

Man's intelligence is insufficient to scoop up the available resources. His intellect needs to be tied to a rope of desire and hard work.

Is your rope – your desire and hard work – in good working condition?

Haircut

"How do you like your hair cut?" the barber asked.

A good barber can cut your hair based on your preference. You walk away satisfied.

When you went for psychotherapy, the doctor asked, "What are the goals that you want to achieve?" You wanted to reduce social phobia, develop assertive skills, and to quit smoking. Being precise with your goals was like telling the barber what haircut you wanted. The therapist could then lead you down that path.

Unless you and the therapist remain mindful of your goals, you could be stuck in therapy forever. So, don't look to your left or right. Set your sights on your goals.

Next Station, Please!

At times I feel like I don't have a goal. I seem aimless, directionless.

Actually, we don't have just one goal. We have an ever-changing 'next goal.'

You have to finish elementary first, then high school, then college, then professional studies. Then there's marriage. Then comes parenthood. Then comes working for your family's financial stability, then supporting the extended family.

The further you go on the highway of life and see new dreams, your goals are refined and you set new goals.

If you feel that you are 'goal-less' at present, it means you've achieved the previous one and are ready for the next one.

Congratulations! Think of your next goal and plan well so you can complete it.

Work Toward a Goal

You went up a staircase and reached the top step. Once at the top, you discovered that there was no landing.

A staircase should take you to a definite place in a building. Your efforts don't amount to anything if there's nothing at the top.

Some people work toward many certifications in small courses. Some go for education, but their goal is only to earn a degree or get a diploma. Though this is better than nothing, it's like reaching the top part of a staircase and finding no floor to step onto. But an education that takes you to something pays off a lot.

For example, someone had taken Medical Terminology. I have nothing against the course, but if he had spent his time getting an accounting degree, it would have been much better for his future.

If he got a BS in Accounting and continued to pursue a certification in Medical Terminology, it would be a positive thing. He could use it somewhere. But if he put his credits toward the next step, a Masters in Accounting, it would pay off way, way more.

Stay focused.

Chapter 44:
Make Peace with the Inevitable

Every Can Has an Expiration Date

My wife, Mahamaya, said that every person born on this earth has an expiration date printed on them.

"We don't have the scanner that can read the exact date of expiry," she added.

All canned food products have expiration dates printed on them. A storage environment with higher temperatures than recommended may spoil the content. For example, the expiration date may be August, but the can's contents may have gone bad by July.

During the Roman Empire, a man's lifespan was thirty years. During World War II, it increased to fifty years, largely because of knowledge about bacteria and the use of antibiotics. The average life span today is 75 years. Knowledge about cholesterol, the standard use of helmets, seatbelts, and vaccines helped greatly.

We can also prolong our lives through regular medical check-ups, exercise, healthy eating, mixing work with play, remaining cheerful, and keeping away from toxic people.

In other circumstances, the can of our life will start spoiling earlier.

In what way?

Through unsafe sex, drug abuse, alcohol abuse, smoking, overworking, and poor money management.

Learn to keep the can of your life in the best atmosphere; otherwise, it will go bad before its expiration date.

The Ultimate Promise

People worry about death. When will I die? How will I die? Why do we die?

The moment a human being is born, there's no telling what will happen in his life or who he will become. However, there is one sure ultimate destination: death.

Consider that a child is born when the parents are 25 years old. It takes 100 years for four generations to be born. Since Jesus Christ, we have had 80 generations. Human beings have been on earth for the last 200 thousand years. That gives us hundreds of thousands of forefathers that died before us.

Since life will likely continue the way it has been, millions of children and grandchildren will come after us. We are part of a process that cannot be broken; therefore, worrying about why death happens and whether it can be stopped is a waste of energy.

Relax and enjoy your short stay on earth. Make the time to look up and see the clouds, breathe fresh air, enjoy the sun's rays, hear the birds, smell the flowers, and feel the raindrops on your skin.

Live life fully, and die without regrets.

Ice Skaters of Time

Anyone who has experienced life will surely taste death. A young child turns into an adult. The unripe becomes ripe. The sun rises in the east and sets in the west. Morning turns to night. Monday becomes Tuesday. These changes don't skip a beat.

Change is constant; therefore I say, "Life is predictable."

However, I would also say that life is unpredictable for each of us. Daily, weekly, monthly, and yearly, the circumstances of our lives change. Our outlook, our responses, our health, and our finances also change, for better or worse. The weather, the stock market, the economy, and even the status of countries change.

We are like ice skaters who have to negotiate our way on the icy surface of time and life. We are ice skaters of time.

Prayer for the Dying

Heart attack. It may cause a person to die in seconds. The suddenness of the departure would leave loved ones grief-stricken, but guilt-free.

It's a different story when an illness strikes and leaves the patient bedridden without the ability to talk or respond.

In this case, caregivers may have any of these responses: "I hope she dies so that she will no longer suffer."

When death comes to the patient, she may have a sense of guilt. "She died because of my wish," she may say.

"I hope she dies so that both of us will cease suffering."

Depression may strike the caregiver. She may be angry toward a higher power who, in her eyes, is the creator of her present situation.

Confusion is always present in these circumstances. The caregiver usually doesn't know how to talk to a higher power.

In Hindi, the term *Mukti* means freedom of the soul from the tattered, old, and disease-wrecked body, to go into a new body and a new life. It's like changing worn out clothing for a new set. You pray to the higher power to release the soul to the next step.

Praying for *Mukti* or salvation of the patient will make the human heart more comfortable; otherwise, the wishing and yearning for the patient to die could only deepen guilt and suffering.

Chapter 45:
Vigilance is Highly Rewarded

Watch the Energy Tank

I glanced at my gasoline indicator.

"Oh my, it's yellow! I still have a long way to go, but my gas tank will be empty soon. I could be stranded on the highway on this dark winter night. I have to find a gas station fast!" I was panicky.

Though the car's GPS helped, it took me 30 minutes before I reached a gas station. For every yard of distance I was saying, "Please, yellow, don't turn red!"

I went through this stress because I hadn't kept an eye on my fuel gauge.

We depend on our husband, wife, son, daughter, or workers. We need to watch and check *their* energy gauges to see whether they're overworked or not.

A chain of behavior follows over-exhaustion. Delay in waking up, tardiness at work, frequent absences, and frequent sick leave are signals that someone is overworked. If left unattended, it will lead to depression, alcoholism, or poor quality of work. In the household, lack of conversation, laughter, intimacy, and impatience are indicators of low energy.

Watch your loved ones' energy gauges. It will keep you from unnecessary and troublesome headaches.

Intentions

Are you aiming to reach your destination without meeting an accident on the highway? If so, be alert. Keep your eyes wide open to the intentions of motorists around you.

The brake lights of the car ahead indicate that the driver is slowing down. Your rearview mirror shows that the car behind you is aggressively moving forward. If he's too close, keep a longer braking distance from the car in front of you. Your side-view mirror tells you whether a car is going to change lanes or cut in front of you. Observe how active the highway patrol is, too.

The more alert you are on the road, the safer you are because you can perform preventive maneuvers.

On the highway of life, watch the behavior and words of your family members, friends, co-workers, bosses, and neighbors. They may have good or bad intentions. Most intentions have nothing to do with you; some minimally affect you. Observation is only possible if you frequently socialize with them. Most of the time, people have no intention to harm, but being watchful will help you better master your social environment.

Use it Before it Fogs Up

I installed a bathroom mirror, but it had a problem: it fogged up quickly. I have to shave and brush prior to showering. I would use the mirror outside the bathroom after my shower.

Thomas is a good friend. He's fun and easy to get along with, but he has a weakness: his mind gets foggy after four drinks. He behaves out of character. Silly laughter replaces his sharp, intelligent speech.

I enjoyed our talks at parties. Knowing his limitations, I would sit with him before he drank. As soon as he started his first round of drinks, that was my cue. I would circulate to the other guests.

I always got the best out of Thomas' company through the right timing—before he fogs up.

This situation can happen to your wife during PMS or your boss during deadlines. Be alert. Take care of potential problems before the situation fogs up.

Freedom to Criticize

When the husband is driving the car, the wife is in the passenger seat. When the wife is driving, the husband is in the passenger seat.

This physical situation is one of the most common sources of arguments between husbands and wives.

"We're in a 25-miles-an-hour zone; slow down."

"You're too close to the car ahead."

"Change lanes."

"You ran a red light."

The driver feels criticized upon hearing these comments.

"Why don't you shut up?" he snaps.

The passenger feels upset.

Why doesn't he listen to me?

Their moods are ruined before they even reach their destination.

My wife and I resolved this problem 35 years ago. It happened like this....

I was driving on a highway. Half of the body of an immobile car was in the right lane. It was jacked up. Somebody was changing its tire.

"There's a car! There's a car!" my wife screamed and startled me to alertness. I hadn't seen the car. I would have hit it and killed the man if not for her warning. During those days, seatbelts were not compulsory yet. My wife and I would have been casualties, too.

I'm a careful, defensive driver. From that time on, I opened myself up to whatever my passenger wanted to say. Off and on, my wife would say something that averted a disaster. It also happened vice versa.

Both of us recognized that we could have our weak moments on the road, so it was possible to make mistakes. We weren't criticizing, but saving each other's lives. I've learned to thank her when she tells me something. She does the same.

Simply put, without getting sour, I have learned to let go of the 19 warnings which were not applicable, and pick up that life-saving *one*.

The Law of Diminishing Return

Wikipedia states, "In economics, diminishing return is the decrease in the marginal output of a production process as the amount of a single factor of production is incrementally increased, while the amounts of all other factors of production stay constant."

Manure gives you better vegetables, but putting one more bag of fertilizer wouldn't do more. A spoonful of sugar in a cup of coffee makes it taste good, but putting more sugar would make it syrupy.

You always spend two hours cleaning your house. It doesn't matter if your house looks perfect. Put in an average number of hours for house cleaning.

In human relationships, spending time together, chatting on the phone, and dining out make a friendship warmer. However, an excess of it would cease to be beneficial; it may become a breeding ground for contempt.

Check who you are relating with before investing your time and effort. Remember the law of diminishing return.

Chapter 46:
Communicate Effectively

Ineffective Noises and Voices of Revolution

Jena is a nurse in a busy section of the hospital. Every time she gets upset with a colleague, her face grows red and her eyes squint. She looks at the person with a hand on her hip, expecting them to know what she's feeling. That's all she does. That was her communication.

Then at lunchtime, she would sit down at the table and tell others how aggravated she was with the person in question, blah, blah, blah.

Her complaints would reach the ears of the subject. A confrontation would follow. It was filled with anger and yelling. It started a cycle of ineffective noises.

On the other hand, Glenda would just walk quietly and calmly away from the scene when she got angry. At lunchtime, she would request to speak privately with the other person. She would point out the specific action that was the source of her anger. She would then ask the person politely not to do the same again. Generally, she gets a good reception from people. Her conversation is without anger. Hers is a voice of revolution.

Which one are you using—a noise or a voice?

Correct Number Dialed Wrong

A husband came home late. The wife was very distraught.

"You came home late. You don't love me," she said.

An argument started.

"How can you say that? Why do you equate my love with my coming home on time or coming home late? That's shallow!" he said irritably.

The fact was that she was missing him a great deal as time stretched on. Instead of saying, "I missed you like crazy, and your lateness made me insecure," it came out differently.

If she was able to articulate her feelings, would he be able to respond accordingly?

You bet.

I can explain it like this.

A patient gave me his phone number. One day I dialed it. It was a non-functioning number.

Did my mind and finger synchronize? Did I read the number right? Did I dial correctly?

I re-read it and re-dialed the number. Bingo! I'd missed a number.

If it's possible for the finger to miss the command from the brain, it's highly possible for two separate individuals to confuse communication due to wrong word usage.

Just like I had dialed one number wrong, misplaced or inappropriate words in a sentence can create problems.

Be aware. Practice what you want to say so that your words will represent how you *truly* feel.

The Cricket

A cricket entered a house. The person didn't know the cricket's exact location, but its chirp resonated in the house until it got on his nerves.

Let's take Ricky as an example. He was dating Ashley but lost interest in her. He stopped returning her calls instead of being forthright about it.

The thought of Ashley kept pestering his mind. It bothered him even when he was out dating another woman.

Finally, he recognized the problem. He phoned Ashley, who felt the same way he did. Both of them were relieved. Closure was official and they remained friends.

An unresolved issue or problem is like a cricket's chirp in the mind. It takes away your peace unless you kill the mental cricket.

You can kill a cricket with bug spray. You can get rid of your mental cricket, the noise of conscience, by resolving an issue.

Chapter 47:
Dating, Inc.

Hair Softener or Chewing Gum

Peter complained. His latest girlfriend, just like his past girlfriends, had quickly broken up with him. He sent her cards, flowers, and chocolates. He helped her with her children. He went to her workplace to take her out to lunch. In spite of all of this, she wanted to date other men.

There are two approaches to relationships. One, be like chewing gum. Have you seen gum stuck in someone's hair? It gets stuck so strongly that the hair gets tangled. Some hair has to be cut off to get rid of the gum. Two, be like a hair softener that gives the hair silky smoothness. Each smooth strand easily separates from another strand, making the hair easy to comb.

Some problems in relationships stem from *too much* contact. We often hear people say that too much familiarity breeds contempt.

Evaluate yourself with this question: Am I like chewing gum or hair softener in this woman's hair?

Hold the Medical History

"I have depression. I'm taking several medications. I'm jobless at present. I hate my family. No one will hire me. Life is hopeless."

Was Daniel talking with his doctor? No.
With his therapist? No.
With his mother? No.
With a buddy? No.
Then who?
His 'romantic date!'

Divulging negative things about yourself is like garbage strewn around. Realize how it might feel sitting on the other side of the conversation.

Make believe that you're dating a girl.

"I'm presently undergoing treatment for my irritable bowel. I might need to step out to the bathroom later," she said. She proceeded to talk about problems with her family. She was so open and comfortable with you that you felt like a priest in a confessional.

You were turned off by this, so you decided not to date her again.

Scattered trash destroys the environment. It's an ugly sight. However, garbage inside a well-covered, painted trash can doesn't distract.

Learn the proper timing for limited self-revelation. It's self-defeating at such an early stage.

Why?

Your relationship with her has no roots yet. A deluge of trash will easily wash out whatever little sign of life there is at that point. Let the friendship show some signs of 'cement' first.

Reveal things about yourself if it serves a necessary purpose. It's good because it shows your honesty and self-acceptance. Self-revelation about your health and problems should never be the focus of a social chat or date.

Natural May Stink

Let's say you're chatting with your girlfriend about your financial woes and struggles with your family and job. You're setting the topic for the evening when you talk about problems. You have relegated fun topics to the background when you focus only on problems.

"Talk less about bad stuff in your life," I told you.

"I feel like I'm being dishonest when I don't tell my friend about my personal problems," you replied.

"Do you use the toilet in front of your partner?"

"Of course not. That would be such a turn-off."

"Do you brush your teeth before you kiss her in the morning?"

"Of course I do."

"Do you apply deodorant so that she can't smell your natural scent?"

"I always do."

"You care for your partner. You clean the rest of your body and spray on cologne for a pleasant smell. You do all those unnatural things because you care, so how come you are verbally so foul?"

"Is it wrong to be honest with my partner about my struggles?"

"Of course not, but don't get too absorbed in the problems in your life. Set limits. If you don't, instead of enjoying each other's company, your togetherness will degenerate into a bitching session. Negatives beget negatives; positives beget positives. Bring in the positives around you so that it's fun to be with you."

How Much Selection?

I received a letter six months back. It was from someone I knew 40 years ago. The letter said:

"Dear Dr. Malhotra, I found you on Facebook after 40 years. I used to work with you as a nurse. I told you about a gentleman who was interested and wanted to marry me. I told you that he was perfect in every way except I didn't love him.

"You told me, 'Most marriages in India were arranged. Parents find partners for their sons or daughters in similar socio-economic class, religion, family constellation, and cultural background. The couples fall in love as time passes.'

"I was in my late 40s. I had waited too long. I was encouraged by what you said, so I decided to say 'yes' to the man.

"He became my husband. I have learned to love him. We've been married 30 years now. It was the best decision that I ever made. I thank you for that conversation."

Today, men and women go on different dating websites in search of partners. They go crazy looking at thousands of choices. Their search for the perfect match becomes exhausting. These people reach their fifties and are still unmarried. Many give up looking.

If you're in a similar situation, recognize that your search should be realistic. Stop fantasizing about meeting the 'perfect partner.' Make your decision based on similarities of religion, culture, habits, and family background. More similarities mean fewer arguments.

Best of luck!

Chapter 48:
Curb Your OCD

Compulsive Shopping

When my wife and I started our married life, we did many things which were outright thrilling. They included rising early in the morning before our fellow apartment dwellers were up. We rummaged through their garbage cans to take out wire hangers that we could use, or furniture that could fill our empty apartment. We leafed through discarded magazines to cut out coupons. On Sunday mornings, we traveled to distant outlets where diapers were on sale. We discussed ways to save a dollar with our friends, who were poor like us. That was our reality then.

Years passed and our financial situation improved. We were able to buy everything that we needed. We cut down on buying things, especially going to sale events.

However, every time we saw a 'garage sale' sign, we would stop the car and join the throng of buyers. Our house was already bursting at the seams. We no longer needed anything. So what were we doing?

I resisted it by saying, "It's not a garage sale. It's a garbage sale. Do I still want to stop the car?"

That was the way I beat the habit.

Do you really need the things that you bought or are planning to buy? The worthiness of the purchase is determined by its usefulness.

Whenever you pick something up, ask yourself, "Is it worth buying or is it a compulsive habit?"

If the answer is, "I need it," go ahead.

If you say, "It's not necessary," yet you end up buying it, putting it in your garage, and forgetting about it, ask yourself, "Have I developed a habit of compulsive shopping?"

The more you challenge it and run away from it, the less power it will have over you.

Obsessively Punctual

Ron was a taskmaster in his household. He made everybody go to bed and wake up early so they would get to school on time. When they were scheduled to go to the beach, he would harp on his family to be up early so they could beat traffic and reach the beach on time. Once they were at the beach, he would nag about leaving on time so they would reach home on time. In the bedroom, he would make love in a rush.

Finally, Ron became aware that something must be wrong with him when he put even his lovemaking under his 'punctual' standard of action. He realized that being on time has its advantages, but pushing it to an extreme is self-defeating.

He started to resist this habit by biting his tongue and not vocalizing, "Hurry up. Let's move it."

Today, the family enjoys their stay at the beach without Ron's 'on-the-dot-watch-clock.' When they were late returning home, the waiting was drowned out by merry laughter in the car.

Nitpicking

Martha has a habit. She visited my office one day, sat down, and her roving eyes went over to my bookshelf.

"Excuse me," she said as she stood up and rearranged my books.

Satisfied, she sat down. Then she noticed my certificates on the wall.

"Excuse me," she said as she jumped up and performed a balancing act with the frames on the wall. She looked satisfied and went back to her seat.

The bookshelf appeared organized and tidy, and the framed certificates seemed balanced. However, before she did her thing on my things, I could find my books without a problem and read my uneven certificates. In short, her actions did nothing to improve the quality of my life.

She was also active in correcting people as they spoke to her.

When somebody told a joke, she would comment that she had heard a different version.

She knows that she has obsessive/compulsive disorder, but people don't perceive it that way. They call her critical and a nuisance, an intrusive person who goes into people's homes and 'fixes' everything.

Are you someone who gets restless when there's a slight variation in the order of things? Ask yourself, "Can life go on without me fixing this?" If your honest answer is 'yes,' stay still, relax, and chill out.

Shut Off the Idling Car

If you're concerned about wasting gasoline, you switch off the car when you're parked.

Let's apply this to life.

Let's say you were resting on the sofa watching TV. Suddenly, you remembered that you had to check the oven. From the kitchen, you went back to the sofa to resume your TV watching. Your spouse told you to stay still and enjoy the TV show. However, you kept on fiddling with your cell phone.

These are signs of anxiety and restlessness.

How do you stop it?

Do exactly what you did to the idling car—switch off its engine.

How do you do that with your body?

Decide to rest and relax. Lay on the sofa, watch TV, or read a book or magazine. While you're at it, there will probably be many thoughts that cross your mind, like checking your emails or other busy tasks.

Ask yourself, "Is it so important that I can't postpone it?"

Remind yourself and say, "This is my rest time. My relaxation is more important than undone tasks."

It can be done if you discipline yourself not to budge.

Chapter 49:
A Light in the Darkness

Fuse Box and Wiring Problems

Electrical problems in the house may be localized or generalized.

One example of a localized problem: the light bulb in your kitchen was out. You changed it and the problem was gone.

An example of a generalized problem: the light bulbs in all the rooms were out. The electrical watches in your house showed the wrong time. Food in your refrigerator spoiled.

You tried to fix them. Some light bulbs worked, some didn't. The electrical watch in the kitchen worked, the one in the bedroom didn't. The refrigerator's temperature was not stable.

Your spouse called an electrician. The root of the problem turned out to be old wiring.

The electrician changed the wiring and everything worked again.

There are two kinds of ailments in the human body. One may be localized arthritis pain in your knee. It can be treated with steroid injections. Another may be a generalized illness like diabetes, high blood pressure, depression, or anxiety disorder. The problem is felt in many parts of the body.

With depression, a person complains of tiredness, hopelessness, sleeplessness, lack of appetite, social withdrawal, crying, irritability, difficulty in concentration, and chronic pain. It seems the house lights are all flickering, the refrigerator isn't working, and the electrical watches are off.

In this condition, giving medicine for the pain in your knee joint alone isn't going to work. Taking care of the fuse box and wiring of the body will address the problem. The fuse box and the wiring is the brain where serotonin and other neurotransmitters help to regulate its activity.

In the case of multiple body symptoms due to depression, antidepressants could manage the fuse box of the brain.

Either/Or

You ask, "Does my depression come from external events or from my personality?"

The workers' insurance company asks, "Does the patient's condition come from his past illness or is it a new injury that occurred on the job?"

If the condition was caused by a combination of factors, it's difficult to communicate it to insurance personnel.

The following metaphor would help them understand the combination effect of two factors that caused the illness.

A person lifted buckets of cement at his job. He worked without any problem for ten years. He developed osteoporosis or porous bones due to nutritional deficiency.

One day, when he lifted the same bucket he had been lifting for ten years, his vertebrae collapsed. He developed disabling back pain.

The question is, "What caused his vertebrae to break? Is it the osteoporosis, which has been developing for the last few months, but didn't prevent him from working and moving on with his life? Is it the bucket that he picked up on the job?"

Well, it's a combination of both. If he hadn't picked up the bucket, he would have been fine. On the other hand, if his bones were in good health, he could have carried the bucket without any problem.

The physical metaphor about the bones and bucket is easy to understand. Let's explore psychiatric symptoms.

A worker was doing very well in his work until he witnessed a fellow worker being crushed and killed. He developed post-traumatic stress disorder.

The post-traumatic stress disorder is like osteoporosis of the emotions. He is depressed and nervous most of the time. He breaks down easily. He can no longer take the stress of the job, which he was able to bear before witnessing the tragedy.

The metaphor of the ordinary bucket breaking the bone makes it easy to understand the cause and effect. Similarly, psychiatric illness can make a worker vulnerable to breakdowns, even if they're due to average stresses.

The Bitter Sauce

"I've been very depressed, down, and desperate. I'm doing my best to decrease my depression, but lots of nasty things have happened in my life."

If the sauce is bitter because of excessive salt, it will be difficult to take the salt out of it. The only way to decrease the salt in the sauce is to add water, potatoes, tomatoes, onions, or other ingredients. When you keep adding to it, the salt becomes diluted. Ultimately, the sauce will become palatable.

If you are depressed because of unpleasant and painful events, add things to your life that bring you joy. Attend a wedding. Go for a walk. Visit friends. Invite your friends to visit you. Go to street fairs. Pick up the phone, call some friends, and have a chat. Go to a movie. Join adult education and training.

Keep on adding things that you can afford as far as time, effort, and energy are concerned. These additives will make your depression diluted and tolerable.

Train to Heaven

Kristin came to my office for treatment of depression after her husband's death. He was the only man she knew and she was completely dependent on him. Taking care of Kristin exhausted her daughter.

Kristin cried and repeated, "I want to kill myself. I want to be with my husband in heaven."

"How do you know there is a heaven?" I asked.

She said without flinching, "I'm Catholic. I know there's a heaven and my husband is there."

"What does your religion teach you about committing suicide? Where would you be?" I proceeded to ask her.

Her daughter jumped in. "According to the Catholic teachings, suicide is a mortal sin."

I explained, "After you die you will get into a train that may take you to hell or to the door of heaven. If you take your own life, your train may not go in heaven's direction; therefore, you're not going to see your husband. In short, going to heaven isn't your sole decision. Your train may take you somewhere else."

She stopped crying and said, "I'll think about that."

The Three Steps of Psychiatric Treatment

Rose, a mother of two children under ten years old, came in with severe depression. She attempted suicide after her husband left her for another woman.

"How can you help me?" she asked, nervously pulling at the cuticles on her nails.

I gave her the metaphor of a house on fire.

First step: run out of your house and call the fire department.

You're depressed and suicidal; your mental house is on fire. Deal with the crisis. Get out of this burning situation that makes you think of suicide. Go into a safe environment like with your family or to a hospital to recover from depression and hopelessness.

Second step: repair what was damaged.

Do soul-searching during the sessions. If the husband helps, great. If he doesn't, take him to court. Join a group for separated/divorced people and learn how to live a single parent life—financially, socially, and even romantically.

Third step: remodel the house and take preventive measures.

Go to psychotherapy sessions. Re-evaluate your thoughts and emotions about yourself as a wife, mother, daughter, and breadwinner. Find out ways of becoming independent economically and socially.

Before you met your husband, you were living a happy life. That life can still be possible. You can be a full person again. It's not an easy journey, but it *is* attainable.

Prisoner of Your Past

Renee remains depressed. She doesn't meet with friends. She works part-time without interaction with coworkers. She shuns family gatherings. If she opens her mouth, it's to talk about tragedies in her childhood: abuse and molestation. She thinks about suicide. To her, life is worthless. She used to read books and crochet, but even the activities she once cherished don't please her anymore.

"Why did you stop these hobbies?" I asked.

"I lost interest," she replied.

"How about developing new hobbies and new friends?"

"It's no use. I don't want to get hurt again."

Renee has created a jail cell made of her childhood hurts. She has locked herself within it for safety. Worse, she refuses to come out of that cage to walk into the open air of the present.

It's not impossible to break the prison walls of the past. But first, the prisoner herself must resolve to get out. Second, a mental health professional can come in to guide her (not coerce her) out of there. The determination of the patient and the efficiency of the physician could turn her from a vulnerable child into an able grownup.

Reframing Perspectives

Angela's mom died seven years ago. Her dad followed three years later.

The loss left a gaping hole in her heart. She wanted to keep that hole because it was where she hid her parents. She visited the hole whenever she felt sad and lonely.

"What if you establish two thrones in your heart? One is for your dad and one is for your mother," I recommended. "When you go talk to them, visualize an impressive, magnificent castle fit for royalty," I added.

Angela liked the idea. She turned the dark hole in her heart into a palace dazzling with extravagant colors for her parents. Her mood and frame of mind changed because there's a vast difference between a royal chamber and a dungeon of sadness.

Don't Jump Into the Well of the Past

Cobwebs covered an empty well. They blocked the sunshine. Worms, rats, bats, cockroaches, and snakes lived there.

Emotional and sexual abuse, bullying, and painful interactions with loved ones are the haunting pain of your past. When you continue to replay these sad events in your mind, it's like jumping into an empty, dark well. The rats, worms, snakes, and cockroaches of your negative experiences are always ready to welcome and consume you. Eventually, you may consider suicide as your way out of that well because its darkness hides the beauty of the outside world from you.

Open your eyes. Can't you see? The darkness inside cannot compare with the beauty outside.

Don't jump into the well again. Keep reminding yourself: "What can an empty, dark well offer me? Darkness and misery— that's all."

A word of caution: the well of the past isn't going anywhere. It will *always* be inside you. But now there's a difference: you're not jumping in.

Counter the painful thoughts of the past by saying, "I'm staying here so I can see the trees and the peaceful sky. I'm staying out of the well so I can be in my garden to pick ripe tomatoes and fruits. I'm staying above ground to feel the sunlight and the raindrops on my skin. I'm staying to hear the birds and the sounds of falling rain. I'm staying outside to smell the fragrance of flowers and freshly baked cookies."

Always be aware of the beauty of the present life around you. It's a potent antidote to the faint force of the well of ugly memories.

Rejuvenate Your Old Garden

Clara's life was full of friends from her high school and college days. She fell in love, got married, and was busy in a happy relationship. She had lost contact with her circle of friends.

When she became a mom of two children, she grew more isolated. One child had a chronic health problem. She left her job to attend to him. Further, she injured her back and said goodbye to skiing.

Time passed by. Once grown up, the children no longer needed her attention. Clara was depressed. She felt that she had no real friends. Her depression came from boredom, loneliness, and feeling worthless.

This was my conversation with Clara.

"You have a nice backyard garden. You've neglected it for a long time because of time constraints. What would you do if you had plenty of time?" I asked.

"Well, I could go to my backyard and check my perennial plants hidden behind the tall bushes," she replied.

"What would you do?"

"I would clear the grass out. Whatever living plant I find I will dig around to make the ground soft. Water is soon to follow."

"Do you know the names of your five best friends in high school and five best friends in college?"

"Yes."

"Find them on the internet and through their family members. Dig them out with emails, Facebook, and phone calls."

She got in touch with them after thirty years. They all responded with delight except for one. Most of them were experiencing the same social isolation. Their phone lines began to burn hot with hours of reminiscing. They stayed in touch on Facebook as well as through emails. She also found out that there was a group account of her high school and middle school class on Facebook.

Since Clara renewed contact with her friends, I have no longer heard her complain about being depressed.

Enjoy the Hotel Lobby

"My girlfriend died of a heart attack a year ago. I saw a sick cat shot by a police officer. These traumatic events keep on replaying in my mind. What should I do?" Luke, who was crying, asked.

I said, "Luke, make believe that you're in the air-conditioned lobby of a hotel. It has huge chandeliers and Persian rugs. You can sit in its cozy atmosphere as long as you want. There are four rooms at the rear for garbage collection. Of course, when waste is present, foul air is present, too. You went out of the lobby to roam around the hotel and ended up in those garbage rooms. Your day was spoiled."

I continued, "My question is: where would you like to spend your spare time? In the garbage room or in the lobby?"

Luke laughed and said, "In the lobby, of course."

I reminded him of his original problem. "We also have a lobby and a garbage room in our mental lives. Your garbage room today is full of the smell of the death of a loved one and the sick cat shot by the police officer. You said you wanted to spend time in the lobby. Good choice. Therefore, avoid going in the direction of the garbage room again."

The lobby of your life is full of lively, pretty colors. Recall the beautiful events in your life. They are more numerous than the stinky stuff inside your garbage room.

Enjoy the best of your lobby!

The Residents of the Graveyard

I entered a graveyard and saw the graves of the rich, the poor, the famous, and the unknown.

I took out my special microphone. It's a long rod of iron with a microphone inside a pointed end. I secured it into the ground and spoke into it.

"I'm addressing those who would like to come out. However, there's a condition. You'll have to go to the doctor, pay his co-pay, take pills, get injections, and undergo chemotherapy. You'll have problems with finances and relationships. You will

272

constantly mow your lawn, shovel snow, and argue with the neighbor and your spouse."

The people who came out had been complaining about their problems when they were alive. Once they experienced a boring life in the ground, they couldn't wait to get back to their world full of problems. What a joyous scene it was!

Next time when you grumble about your problems, think twice. If you think of taking your life, remember that in spite of your problems, you can see life in all its grandeur.

We only live once. Hold on to life. The grave calls at the perfect time. Don't be in a hurry to become dust.

Can't Enjoy Dinner

Jasmine was raped when she was nine years old. She kept it a secret.

She is now married to an affectionate man who cares for her, but she isn't able to enjoy their lovemaking. She can't understand why.

Let me take you to a very good restaurant and offer you good food. Before the food comes, I ask you to imagine pooping on the plate.

Would you be able to enjoy the meal?

No, though the food is delicious and served nicely.

Why?

Your mind is picturing the poop on your plate. It's a repulsive vision that takes the joy out of a good meal. You know that the poop is just in your head, yet you can't eat the food.

At night, it's time to make love to your spouse. You thought of the rapist doing the same that your husband is doing. This is like visualizing poop on your dinner plate, so it turns you off.

How can you make the thought go away?

Talk to yourself. Repeatedly say, "It's not real. It was in the past, and the past is dead. It's just a thought and a thought is not real."

Then focus on what your partner is saying and doing. Constantly focus on something else other than the thought of the poop on your plate.

When you focus on one thought in your head, it inhibits other thoughts. Like you're drinking a glass of air but you want the air out. Fill the glass with water and the air will automatically come out.

These thoughts are like the air in the glass. When you start singing, whistling, praying, or doing jumping jacks, the air will come out. Repeatedly filling the glass with many diversionary tactics will wipe out the bad thoughts. You will see improvement in your response to intimate moments with your husband.

Trash it or Save It

Doreen: "I lost my job for the second time. I'm useless and worthless. I'm good for nothing. I'm thinking of committing suicide."

Doctor: "Let's make believe that you had a collision with another vehicle. Your car was badly damaged. The insurance refused repair. You think they're right. What would you do with your car?"

Doreen: "I would give it to the junkyard."

Doctor: "Do you know what junkyards do with these cars?"

Doreen: "No. Maybe they use the good parts?"

Doctor: "They sell them. There's a market for used car parts. People need them. Do you know that a good car door costs $500-$600? A backseat without damage would go for $500. Tires in good shape are bought by some garages."

Doreen: "I guess you're right. I heard that a car is worth much more if sold in parts."

Doctor: "A damaged car on the side of the road isn't worth a penny, but it's worth hundreds of dollars once it's in the junkyard. Have we established that?"

Doreen: "Yes."

Doctor: "Now, would you burn your car or abandon it where it lay, or would you give it to the junkyard?"

Doreen: "I would give it to the junkyard."

Doctor: "Your previous job can no longer use you. It feels like you're a damaged, useless car. Killing yourself is like burning your car. Surrendering to your situation without a fight is like abandoning your car on the side of the road. Going to the junkyard means looking for another job. Maybe others will find that your skills are fitting to their needs."

Doreen: "I guess you're right. I gave up too soon. I'm going to start looking for a new job."

Real Psychotherapy

Jean developed a seizure disorder, epilepsy. She lost her license to drive for six months. It was the required period for observation. Another attack of epilepsy would prolong the suspension period.

Jean is holding a good, well-paid job. She loves going to work. She's never been sick for an extended period during her years of employment. The thought of staying at home always makes her anxious and depressed.

"My job inspires me so much. Reporting to my office every day is like going to a psychotherapy session," she said.

Her question was, "Should I spend $40 a day for cab fare to work or should I take six months off and go for counseling for depression due to loneliness?"

"Go to your 'real' psychotherapy session—your work," I advised.

She exhaled a sigh of relief. A smile and a vigorous nod showed her happy agreement with what she heard. A $40 cab fare was a much better investment than going to psychotherapy for depression caused by lack of work.

Chapter 50:
Shake Off Your Addiction

Don't Flag Down the Cab

A patient of mine, PW, had abused narcotics.

"How do you resist the urge to abuse narcotics?" I asked during his recovery.

"I make believe that the urge is like a passing cab. I can choose to flag it down or let it go. I don't focus on the cab; I focus on what I have to do. I let the thought of taking narcotics pass. Once I do that, there's no cab that I can get into."

Immediate Effect and Delayed Effect

Every action results in immediate and delayed effects. Unfortunately, it's the immediate effect that dominates.

One example is using a credit card versus cash. When people pay cash for food, jewelry, or a vacation, the pain of spending money is so much that people scale down their spending. But when they swipe a card in the machine, there is no pain. The torment of paying the monthly installments doesn't dominate the moment.

In cigarette smoking, the nicotine gives an immediate sense of well-being. Later effects are breathlessness, lung disease, heart disease, stroke, cancer, and amputated feet. In spite of knowing the complications, the immediate effect of nicotine dominates, making millions of people dependent on cigarettes.

Whenever you act, ask what the immediate positive and negative effects are as well as the delayed positive and negative effects. Then choose what's more beneficial to you in the long run.

Layers of Problems and Solutions

Let's say you saw a burning house. The firemen put it out with water. Then they went inside to check for any embers that might reignite the fire.

Then came the cleanup of debris. Once that was done, the damaged parts were replaced.

Finally, painting begun. It made the house look as if it was never on fire.

The same goes for people who are experiencing severe emotional problems, drug abuse, or alcoholism. Their life is on fire.

Let's suppose somebody has decided to quit taking drugs. He cuts down on heroin. The flame is less because he's still smoking marijuana. It was a three-alarm fire before, but it was reduced to a two-alarm fire. Then he cuts down on marijuana, but he's still jobless. Then he harnesses his skills and gets back to where he left off in college.

Everything happens in layers. The house on fire didn't get fully repaired in just a day. The chaos of drug addiction won't improve with a snap of your fingers. It happens one phase at a time.

Recognizing the layers is important. It gives you a feeling of victory, knowing that you have come from such a low place and hurdled such hard stuff, and knowing where you are today.

Let the Cactus Die of Neglect

Do you want to get rid of a thorny cactus in your backyard?

There are two ways of dealing with it. One, you uproot and take it out. This option is hard because you have to deal with its thorns. Two, you totally neglect it. You cover it with plastic so it doesn't get air, sunshine, or water. It would die on its own.

Certain relationships in our life can be taken care of through neglect.

Let's say that you have friends whose weekend activity is drinking. You all gather around a table full of alcohol. Every person encourages the others to have one more glass and another. If you cut down your intake, they make fun of you. They don't let anybody escape until the last drop is gone. If you say, "Let's take it slow," they see it as a 'sermon' they don't want to hear.

If you don't want to be trapped in alcohol, neglect your drinking buddies. Put plastic covering on the relationships by declining their invitations. Eventually, they will lose interest in you and you will lose interest in them.

AA and NA Vitamins

There are support groups for alcoholism and drug addiction called Alcoholics Anonymous and Narcotics Anonymous, nicknamed AA and NA. I always suggest this 12-step program along with other treatments. I give the following example when the patient doesn't show interest.

There are two kinds of pills. One type fights the disease itself. Another type is like vitamins that strengthen the body to combat the disease.

Alcoholics Anonymous, Narcotics Anonymous, and other 12-step programs are like vitamins. They sustain you throughout your fight against your addiction. They help you live a balanced life. Your wellness will become such that you'll never need the support of alcohol or drugs ever again.

From Scotch to Wine

Matt used to drink scotch excessively. He agreed that instead of drinking scotch, he would drink wine. His alcohol consumption was less for a while because wine has less alcohol concentration than scotch.

As time passed, things started to change. Matt drank more wine in volume. A small glass of scotch is equal to a glass of wine or a large mug of beer in its alcohol content. He got tipsy and his voice became unclear every time he drank excess wine.

Matt was like someone who gambled on the dollar slot machine in a casino. He was losing. He transferred his play to a quarter slot machine. He found out that he could bet six quarters or a total of $1.50. He spent a dollar in a dollar slot machine before, but he now put six quarters in the quarter slot machine. He would be spending more money even if he shifted to a lower denomination slot machine. In other words, Matt is now taking more alcohol into his system even though he moved to a less concentrated drink.

The real problem isn't the kind of alcohol a person drinks, but the total amount of alcohol he consumes.

Don't Throw Gasoline on a Burning House

A person who has severe mental illness like schizophrenia, bipolar disorder, panic disorder, or major depression is like a house on fire. You should take these diseases seriously.

If you throw gasoline on a burning house instead of calling the fire department, the house will be gutted. If you call the fire department but keep throwing gasoline on the fire, it will overpower the water. The fire will consume the house.

The gasoline I'm referring to is illegal drugs and alcohol.

The brain cannot tolerate two attacks at the same time—the major illness and the element that worsens the disease.

If you want to save your house, call the fire department. Obviously, that means get medical help. Then throw water on the house, i.e. take your medicine. Stay away from alcohol and drugs. They're like gasoline, making the fire burn uncontrollably.

Preventive Maintenance

Ben said, "I've been sober for one year, so I stopped going to AA meetings. It's so difficult to make the time."

"Spending a couple of hours in Alcoholics Anonymous is an investment to prevent a relapse. If you don't practice preventive maintenance of your car, it can break down when you least expect it. You lose self-esteem, work days, and relationships."

When we pay insurance premiums, we think that it's a waste of money. "I could have used the money for something else," we say. However, the time you spend in AA meetings serves as your insurance premium.

I recommend that if you have a problem with alcohol, drugs, gambling, sex addiction, or domestic violence, please invest time in your support group.

Flash Point

A waiter brought food to your table, poured some brandy on the food, lit a match, and voila! A two- to three-foot controlled fire suddenly flared up.

Some people gasped in surprise. Some were jolted to defensive poses. Others shrieked with delight and laughter. That was the whole idea. Then the food was served and everybody ate. The fire didn't contribute any special taste to the food, but the event prior to eating gave the element of surprise and drama to everyone in the restaurant.

What alcohol did on the food is what it does to a person. Anger, violence, suicide, and other negative emotions are often stirred by alcohol. They rise like the two- to three-foot tall flame in the person.

An angry person holds his breath and bites his tongue because he recognizes that uncontrolled anger causes more pain than solutions. But when he pours alcohol into his system, he loses control and indiscriminately lashes out at anyone in sight.

There are people who can keep their violent tendencies under control. But when they submit to alcohol, they become a far cry from the 'calm' person they are known to be. They end up damaging property or breaking people's jaws... and going straight to jail or the hospital.

Some people entertain suicide on and off. But they never attempt it, realizing its futility. However, people could become vulnerable to the idea when they submit to alcohol.

The same is true in some areas of life. Alcohol could cause a two- to three-foot flash of flame without any positive gain.

Waiters were trained to handle this kind of food by the restaurant chef. An untrained waiter would be burned by the flame. However, this isn't true in real life. A person who loves alcohol can never be trained to handle it well. Slowly but surely, he would burn and burn.

Sexy Girl with AIDS

Jake was sober. He had done his last drugs five months before. Occasionally, he was tempted to do them 'just one more time.'

A thought like that is a potential road toward relapse. Jake doesn't think in terms of how long and how much hard work it has taken him to reach where he is. He only thinks of the whiskey's warm, stinging taste in his mouth and stomach. That thought could progress to desiring the other things that he was used to taking. Fleeting gratification grips his mind and he ignores where he's heading.

I was concerned that he was getting close to a relapse. I asked, "A woman is very attractive and sexy. You desire her so much, you want to have sex with her. However, she's honest and tells you that she has AIDS. What would you do?"

Jake started laughing nervously, "I would run away as fast and as far as I can."

I pointed out, "Your alcohol, cocaine, and other narcotics are just like that woman—enticing, yet fatal. You will be paying for that very short time of pleasure with years of suffering and eventual death."

Chapter 51:
Trade Anxiety for Calm

Lack of Tolerance

Imagine that your anxiety attacks were very severe. You were unable to function. You were ready to check yourself into a hospital.

You've come a long way. You have improved over a period of time, but you complained about minor symptoms. You got very upset in spite of the doctor's reassurance. You are very intolerant to any problem.

Your case is similar to this:

You lived in a cluttered house. Magazines, pieces of paper, shoes, and clothes lay around.

"This has to stop. I don't want to live with all this mess," you said. You cleaned up. You turned your place into a spick-and-span dwelling.

Then you walked in one day and saw a shoe lying in one corner of the room.

"Why is that shoe out of the shoe rack? It's getting messy in here," you complained.

You tossed your things everywhere before and called it a mess. A shoe was outside the shoe rack today and you called it a mess. With many symptoms before, you felt sick. With one symptom today, you feel sick.

Firstly, you have grown stronger; your senses have become sharper. An improved person reacts to minor symptoms. Secondly, you're scared that the shoe is the harbinger of a cluttered house. You're afraid of a full-blown anxiety attack.

Anxiety About Driving Far

I live in a suburban town in New Jersey, so I don't drive great distances. One time, a friend from India wanted us to meet in New York.

I was very anxious about driving in congested traffic. However, if my friend could travel from India to the USA, the least I could do was drive from NJ to NY. So there I was, driving alone. I accomplished the trip by talking to myself loudly. Here are a few examples of what I said to myself.

"Driving out of my small street to the highway going to New York is the same as driving out of my street to the bigger road to my office. I have frequently driven on this road," I said when my nervousness wanted to get the better of me.

"It's no big deal. One highway is no different from another highway," I said when my heart started to beat fast, seeing that I wasn't familiar with the road that my GPS was leading me to.

"So what? If I'm taking the wrong exit, my GPS will tell me how to get back on the right road," I said when I was hesitant about heading toward an exit.

When my mind said, "This is very far," I pacified myself with, "It only means sitting in the driver's seat longer. If I can stay in the driver's seat for ten minutes, what's the problem with 45 minutes? No problem."

"It's the same left and right turn that I've always taken except that the street name is new. So, there's no problem," I said when I took a left or a right turn onto an unfamiliar street.

By constantly talking to myself and translating everything into a less sinister thought, my anxiety remained under control. I was not only able to reach New York without incident, but I was able to return home confidently.

Talk Yourself Out of Distraction

Are you anxious and restless? Do you go round and round like the blades of an electric fan?

You sat down to rest after work or dozed off in front of the TV and woke up startled.

Zing! Suddenly you run to take care of a routine job that could be done later. Seeing, hearing, or thinking of something is like 100 volts that makes you jump like a new military recruit.

You would worry about your business while you were sitting at church. It wasn't the business that was distracting you; you were pulling the business into the church.

Distraction comes from within you, not from without. The urge to turn your face and tend to the distraction has become a habit.

Stand your ground. Remind yourself, "I'm restless, but I don't have to be. Distraction has no control over me. I'm enjoying myself on the sofa right now. I'll take care of the task later. I am the master of myself. I shall prevail."

Invest Anxiety to Reduce Anxiety

"Whenever I change the way I do things, I get nervous. New stuff and new people make me nervous. Therefore, I stay in my old habits."

Let's make believe that you have high heating bills because your windows are not energy efficient. You consulted somebody who does energy conservation. He suggested double glazed windows consisting of two layers of glass with a layer of inert gas sealed between them. This creates nearly twice the insulation. However, money is involved in changing to this window type. You have to invest $5,000. Nevertheless, over the years, you would save $40,000 in energy bills.

Some expense is necessary today to avoid incurring big bills in the future. In the same way, tolerating anxiety today is crucial to becoming anxiety-free tomorrow.

Don't be shortsighted. Face new things boldly and tolerate new fear for the sake of future calm.

A Practice Interview

Robin was scared of job interviews. He always seemed to have left his tongue at home. When he was able to open his mouth at last, he would be stammering.

Why was this so? He was anxious about making mistakes and failing.

He made all kinds of excuses not to go. When we talked in detail, I found out that he lacked the needed positive statements to give him confidence. It all boiled down to his predictions of failure and rejection.

I coached him for future interviews.

"Go to the first 20 interviews saying, 'This is a practice interview. If I get the job, swell! If I don't, who cares? I can walk away with more experience for future interviews.'"

No Guillotine

When you're going somewhere and your anxiety starts building up, say to yourself, "I'm not heading toward a guillotine. Nobody is going to chop my head off. The worst thing they can do is refuse me for the job. The worst thing they can say is, 'Don't come to work.' There are other jobs, other places, and other people. If this guy doesn't like me, screw him. I don't care. There is no guillotine, and he isn't the executioner."

Three Meals a Day

Eric was anxious. He was a nervous person.

"Eric, I taught you how to relax. Do you practice the relaxation exercises?" I asked.

Eric threw his hands in the air and replied, "Oh, it's useless. I did them a couple of times. It didn't work. I'm still anxious."

"Do you eat food?" I continued.

Eric said a hesitant, "Yes, I do."

"How long have you been eating?" I asked.

Eric was patient in answering my questions. "Many years. All my life," he said.

Finally, I stressed my point. "When you eat food, it usually lasts for six hours. Then you have to feed yourself again. You can't expect complete freedom from anxiety by exercising once. If you do, it's like saying, 'Though I feel hungry now, I shouldn't eat food again because I ate in the past.'"

When you practice relaxation exercises or meditation for anxiety, tension, and nervousness, it's going to last only for a few hours. Tension starts to build up again when a new situation develops, meaning you have to exercise again.

You never hesitate to eat three meals a day. So please, do your minute-long relaxation exercise three times a day.

Don't Make Mountains Out of Molehills

I have a friend who frets in response to little things. He gets aggravated if someone is two minutes late, there is a slight delay in food service at a restaurant, or if his children make noise and his wife isn't able to control them. He gets aggravated when he doesn't like the presents he receives on Christmas. He says, "They have no gift sense."

This attitude of making mountains out of molehills makes him an unpleasant companion.

It's logical to get upset when a person arrives late for an interview. If a lecture is going on and a child is making noise, the child should be taken outside. However, a major reaction to anything and everything that can be passed off as minor is unnecessary. It's like firing a round of machine gun bullets to kill flies. It's overkill.

If you're easily aggravated, you become too much to bear for the people around you. You're not a joy to be with because people will always be walking on eggshells.

When you're tempted to feel bothered, ask yourself, "Is this a legitimate mountain, or is this a molehill that I want to treat like a mountain?"

Screaming Doesn't Put the Fire Out

Gene called her mother, Mary, to tell her that her house was flooded, causing extensive damage. Gene's financial situation was such that she could work it out. She hoped that the insurance would cover the repairs.

Mary couldn't sleep, rest, or relax after learning what happened. She was so uptight that she was on the brink of drinking again.

"Make believe that your house is on fire. Would jumping, yelling, and screaming put the fire out?" I asked Mary.

"No," she answered.

"What should you do?"

"Call the fire department."

I said, "Exactly. Being edgy and anxious won't help Gene. Your daughter needs the calming effect of your strong arms around her. You wouldn't be able to assist her if you were to relapse into drinking and become a nervous wreck again. Recognize the practical and emotional demands of her situation and ask her how you can help."

Hobbies Give Us Reasons to Live

Thomas was anxious, bored, and nervous. He no longer worked due to a physical disability. His TV set was his only friend and companion. It filled his waking hours. In short, he had a lot of time to agonize over his disability, pain, and frustration.

He used to paint. People bought his art, but he lost interest and stopped altogether.

I told him that his present lifestyle is like a jungle he's stuck in.

I said, "Let's make believe that you're shipwrecked on a deserted island. You don't know if any rescue team will ever find and save you. You found two saplings in the wild—an orange and a mango. What would you do with them?"

His eyes lit up. "I would make sure that I don't trample them."

"Good. What else?" I continued.

"I would nurture them until they become trees that bear fruit. I would eat them, save the seeds, and then plant those. I would have groves of mango and orange trees. They would benefit those who come to the island. Nurturing them would give me a reason to fill my day," he said.

"You wouldn't step on the saplings in the story. In your present state in life, it means that when the saplings, the thought of painting, crosses your mind, don't brush it off. Strive to become a good painter. Having a goal will drive away your boredom and anxiety," I said.

Why is that? Anxiety-producing thoughts don't linger when your mind is occupied with an activity you enjoy. When you want to exercise, make a phone call, or start a business from your house, don't push it away. Your desire could be the sapling of a big business or a flourishing hobby that makes you happy.

What Other People Say

Ears produce wax to preserve the inner lining. Taking a shower washes it out. A Q-tip removes the remaining wax. Clean ears!

On the other hand, when more Q-tips are rubbed in the already clean ear, they become an abrasive that can damage the inner walls of the ear.

Overdoing the cleaning injures the ears. In short, a good habit becomes a damaging habit.

How does this principle work in human relationships?

Brenda's friends like her. She's thoughtful and communicative, but she takes these traits to the extreme. She frets if she doesn't hear from them.

"What did I do? Why are they not communicating?" she asks.

Not able to bear their silence, she calls or sends text messages with a sense of urgency. "Are you okay?" she inquires.

Her friends become aggravated when Brenda repeatedly calls, texts, or emails them to check. They don't respond because they want to keep the repeated calls under control. This makes her persist. She's like the abrasive Q-tip that irritates the ears.

Concern for others is a wonderful attitude, but raising it to an excessive level is like overdoing the ear cleaning. An irritated ear produces more wax and itches, and that would start a vicious cycle of more itching and wax. The result is infection and a visit to the doctor.

"Leave your ears alone," the doctor would say.

Brenda, please slow down and take it easy. Spread your wings through hobbies, education, dancing, or martial arts. Leave your loved ones alone for a few hours so that when they see you again, they're happy to see you and enjoy your company.

Chapter 52:
The Power of Being Still

A Panic Attack is Like Sneezing

Seconds before sneezing, a man's face gets contorted. His eyes close a little bit, his nostrils flare up, and his mouth opens. Depending on how mild or hard the sneeze is, after a little pause, his whole body tenses up. He breathes in loud, then in a definite manner, he sneezes.

"Achooo!"

There are brain centers that control complex behaviors when activated. For example, a sneeze could be triggered by a tickle from a stray dust particle inside the nose. Whatever the cause, the sneeze center – just like the orgasm center, the coughing center, or the vomiting center – of the brain gets activated. Then the sneeze is automatic.

A sneeze doesn't do damage to a person's body. It doesn't create any difficulty with his muscles. It does the job of ejecting a dust particle from his nose.

There are centers in the brain which coordinate the muscles, respiration, heart, and blood pressure during that time. Once you've sneezed or coughed, your physiology normalizes.

A panic attack is similar to sneezing. There's an area in the brain that controls the 'fight or flight' reaction. During job interviews, the heart palpitates, hands get sweaty, and nausea occurs. When the interview is over, the body goes back to normal.

A panic attack is like a sneeze. It's a regular function of the body that occurs at the wrong time. It doesn't do damage to the body and it doesn't create any difficulty with the muscles.

Next time you have a panic attack, say, "My body is going to sneeze."

A Jungle Fire on TV

Make believe that you're watching TV. A jungle fire is spreading fast. People are running frantically. The fire is engulfing houses and trees. It's a horrible scene. It makes your heart palpitate.

However, no matter how intense the fire, it's not going to spread into your house because it's confined to the TV screen. You are 100% safe. Your fear is only there while the program lasts. When it's over, you can turn off the TV and go to sleep.

Panic disorder is a condition in which the fight-flight reaction of the body causes palpitations, muscle tightness, and dizziness. The person has a sense of losing control of his bowels, feeling like passing out, and feeling like he's losing his mind. The person is scared of going crazy, choking to death, or having a heart attack.

If a person happened to be in the elevator during a panic attack, he would avoid elevators from then on. If he happened to be on a train, he would no longer ride trains. If he happened to be driving, he would avoid cars. If he happened to be in a restaurant, he would avoid that specific restaurant. He would start believing that those places caused the attack.

In truth, panic attacks are not related to any place or activity. They happen wherever you are. The anxiety, nervousness, or fear of panic attacks often comes because people are *expecting* an attack: "I will have a panic attack; I'm going to have a panic attack!"

People should be able to differentiate between anxieties caused by a panic attack and the stress caused by repeated fear of the attack itself.

Whenever any of the above-mentioned symptoms occur for the first time, a person should go to the emergency room. The doctor will get a detailed medical history and do blood tests, ECG, x-ray, and medical examinations.

On the other hand, doctors often make the mistake of not telling the patient that he had a panic attack. In so doing, they miss recommending that the patient see a psychiatrist to get educated and medicated. Many doctors are not fully conversant with the management of panic disorder.

Doctors kid around like, "You're healthier than your doctor. Go home, you're okay. Stop worrying."

Then the patient wonders, "Am I going crazy or something?"

Understand that your panic attack is like a jungle fire on the TV screen. It can't destroy you. It can't take your life away. It can't give you a heart attack or a brain tumor. Its symptoms are self-limiting. They don't go beyond the 10-minute maximum, the world record for a panic attack.

During a panic attack, you are going to suffer. But just like watching the fire on TV, you're perfectly safe afterwards. If it continues to bother you, see a psychiatrist.

Chapter 53:
Medicine is a Solution

Repair the Stranded Car

A patient had severe depression. She didn't take the medicine prescribed to her, so her depression continued with the same severity.

"You didn't take your medicine. Why?" I asked the patient.

"I'm not sure whether the medicine will work or not, so I didn't take any of it," she replied.

She was right. There is no guarantee that medicine will work for everybody.

"You have two options if your car is stranded on the road. First, you leave it unattended. Second, you get a mechanic to check the car. There's a possibility that the problem is beyond his ability. But do you think leaving it unattended is the best option rather than asking a repair person to make it okay?" I asked.

She said, "Getting the repair person might be a good idea. Giving him a chance is the best action."

I said, "Please give me and the medicine a chance."

Medication Selection

A blunt knife cuts vegetables and meat with difficulty, but it does not cut your finger. A sharp knife cuts vegetables and meat easily—including your fingers. The sharper the knife, the riskier it is.

How does this relate to your medicine?

A physician prescribes drugs with the least side effects. It may be medication for psychiatric illness, sleep, pain, blood pressure, or diabetes. If the medicine doesn't work, the physician may then prescribe drugs with side effects.

Patients commonly ask for medications that work fast. For example, they ask for narcotics for pain or hypnotics for sleep instead of doing nonchemical relaxation exercises.

The drugs chosen for you are not as active as the sharp knife, but they will help control your illness. The advantage is that there are less side effects, like cutting your hand. If you don't get relief, it's time to try the 'sharper knife.'

Patients, work with your doctor patiently!

Physical Problems Need Physical Medicine

Let's say that a patient has major depression, schizophrenia, panic disorder, bipolar disorder, or dementia. These are all physical illnesses of the brain. In these cases, psychotherapy and talk therapy alone are not going to work. The patient needs medicine, but refuses to take the prescribed medications.

"I want counseling," he says.

If a person has diarrhea, counseling him about diarrhea and stomach pain doesn't cure the problem. He has to take medication to arrest any bacterial growth inside his intestines.

The same is true for brain disorders. Think of them like brain diarrhea. They need physical medicine to treat the illness. Talk and counseling alone won't help.

Don't Wait for a Fire to Go Out on its Own

My patient refused to take medicine for a severe psychiatric illness. He wanted psychotherapy or observation only.

The following metaphor helps.

Doctor: "If your house is on fire, why not just sit and pray?"

Patient: "Are you kidding? My house will burn down!"

Doctor: "In this case, maybe it will just go out without leaving much damage."

Patient: "I'm not going to take any chances. I'll call the fire department."

Doctor: "You're right. If you just let the fire burn, it will damage your house. From my experience and the scientific research I follow, I see that your psychiatric illness is severe, like a house fire. I doubt that your current mental illness will improve on its own or even with psychotherapy. So what do you say? Can you now take your medicine and start throwing water on your psychiatric fire?"

Clouds Blocking the Sunshine

Physical and psychiatric illnesses can be devastating. A person becomes anxious, depressed, and aggravated.

To reduce physical discomfort and pain, the patient has to take medicine. Drugs cause improvement. Infrequently, they have side effects. A few days after chemotherapy, a patient is drained. He probably wants to lay in bed all the time.

The following metaphor never fails to help the patient understand his situation.

If you're suffering the side effects of medicine, think of them as clouds covering the sunshine of health. The side effects may be short-lived. When tiredness, nausea, skin irritation, sleepiness, or muscle cramps subside, you will feel better again.

Taking Sleeping Pills the Correct Way

The doctor's instructions may be unclear, or the patient's understanding may be faulty about taking a sleeping pill.

The doctor instructed the patient to take a sleeping pill before bedtime. Family members kept tabs of his pills. When the patient had fallen asleep without the pill, a family member would wake him up to let him take the sleeping pill.

It was like, "Hey, wake up and take your sleeping pill." Ironic, isn't it?

Clarify with your doctor. Does he want you to take the sleeping pill every night or only as needed?

By the way, sleeping pills are given when the patient *cannot* sleep. Taking the pill even though the person is sleeping well is like using a flashlight in the sun.

Chapter 54:
Patient Compliance Makes a Difference

I Am the Chef of Medicine

Some patients have the boldness to reduce the dose of their medicine on their own.

I recommended that she take 5mg. Next time she came in, she said she took only half the tablet.

"Why?" I asked.

She answered, "Just because."

I asked her, "Imagine you're a chef. You gave me a recipe for spaghetti sauce. You instructed me to put one teaspoon of salt in a pot. However, I only put half a teaspoon. What kind of sauce do you think it will be?"

She smiled and replied, "Well, it won't taste good."

I smiled back and said, "Exactly. I'm the chef who knows the ingredients of the medicine and the amount that would make it curative, in the same way that you know the quantity of elements that would make the sauce tasty. Changing the recipe unless there's a good reason doesn't make sense. So, don't reduce your medicine without talking to me."

Choosing the Right Medicine

Our armamentarium is vast. It is like a shoe store.

A shoe store has every kind of shoe—for jogging, office wear, party, travel, dancing, and sports, to name a few. There are high-heeled shoes, flat shoes, boots, sneakers, gladiator shoes, and others.

However, the topmost goal is to get the best fit for the client's foot. Getting the best fit has some considerations. The client's previous experience with a certain shoe size, type, and style are important. The salesperson may see an ingrown toenail or other problem, so he may suggest a shoe that's broad in the front.

In the same way, medical practitioners have a wide choice of medicines that could best battle the patient's illness. However, to get the best fit, he makes some adjustments based on the patient's previous experience with medicine, his body's tolerance level, and the effect of the medications on him. He also experiments with other drugs to avoid future side effects.

When the patient cooperates with his doctor, together they discover the medicine that fights the illness but doesn't cause side effects.

Slow Detoxification

Sub Oxone medicine has been giving Anne relief from agonizing pain. However, her doctor was concerned that the longer she stays on this narcotic, the more she would suffer due to the medicine's habit-forming side effects. He instructed Anne to cut down the dosage from 8mg to 6mg daily. He planned to reduce it further as her body adjusted to the taper.

This worried Anne. The thought of the pain returning scared her. She hesitated.

"I'm not asking you to promise that you will succeed. *Try* to take 6mg. Just hold the remaining 2mg dose at hand and take it if you can't tolerate the reduction," the doctor said.

Anne agreed to work on reducing Sub Oxone. Her doctor congratulated her for agreeing to try.

Trying is under man's control; succeeding is not. Small and big projects start with trying. Success depends on many variables.

Do You Need a Hearing Aid?

Five years back, I received a phone call from my answering service. The operator had a message for me. She was speaking in a low volume. I couldn't understand what she was saying.

"Did you have breakfast today?" I asked.

"Yes, I did," she replied. "Why do you ask?"

"You're talking so softly. I can barely hear you. It's as if you are weak."

"But this is my normal way of talking."

"Talk a little louder, please."

I didn't pay attention when a few people spoke to me in a whisper-like fashion. But when *all* people seemed to speak to me from a far-away cave, it got my attention. Instead of questioning their volume, it had me investigating my hearing faculty. I went for an ear exam and was prescribed a hearing aid.

How does this apply to our emotional life?

Most often, we're unaware of our own shortcomings that have created difficulties for us.

When people repeatedly bothered you in a certain way, did you ponder your attitude toward it? How did you deal with it? How did you handle yourself?

Not every fault falls on the other party. Value the counsel of a loved one or a trusted friend. Have the strength to say 'no' to your own attitude that hinders your mental, emotional, and physical wellbeing. You may finally understand that submitting yourself to psychotherapy with a professional counselor has been long overdue.

Reversible vs. Irreversible Illnesses

There are two kinds of illness. The first type is a reversible illness. For example:

A fractured leg; after the cast is taken off, the leg goes back to its previous condition. Sore throat or pneumonia; after antibiotics, the person recovers. Food poisoning; once it flushes out of a person's system, he is safe.

These are reversible conditions. The person returns to normal after proper treatment.

The second type is an irreversible illness. For example, diabetes, arthritis, blood pressure, depression, schizophrenia, bipolar disorder, or panic disorder.

They stay. They live with the person. People feel better after a few days of medication. They believe that they're cured. Nevertheless, they may need long-term treatment with psychotherapy, medication, or both.

"I'm tired of taking medicine," they might say, and off to the toilet bowl their medicines go. Their illness relapses.

The nature and type of your illness and the chances of relapse after stopping your medicine are important considerations that you must take. Discuss these things with your doctor before throwing your medicine away. Your wellness is at stake.

Chapter 55:
Psychosis

Rat-Infested House

Imagine that your house was infested with rats. You set up traps and caught some. They repulsed you and made your life miserable. You decided to burn your house down to terminate them all.

Destroying your dwelling is a self-defeating solution to your rat problem. The best solution? Hire an exterminator.

If the rat exterminator couldn't get rid of all the rats, he could educate you about some preventative steps.

The house represents your life, the rats represent your job, relationships, insecurity, and hopelessness. You have tried fixing them but couldn't. The problems seemed intolerable, inescapable, and interminable, so you decided to solve them with suicide.

If you couldn't solve your problems, why not get help from a mental health professional? Mountain-like obstacles for you are molehills for them. They have spent a lifetime learning to understand, analyze, and find solutions. Like the exterminator, if he couldn't entirely solve your problem, he could cut down its intensity, frequency, and duration and make life livable again.

Someone Follows Me

Patient: "Doctor, I think somebody is following me. Wherever I go, I hear these voices. They talk to me, they talk to each other. Even when I'm surrounded by people, I still hear them. I think they're electronically transmitting their voices to me. Why is that?"

Doctor: "I believe you're familiar with a CD player. You hear songs when a CD is played on it, but you know that there's no actual person there. Those are voices of singers brought to your hearing through electronic and magnetic waves."

Liken your head to a CD player. You hear voices that your thoughts play, but these voices don't belong to actual people. They are produced by your mind. But when you go somewhere and leave the CD player at home, you no longer hear the CD sounds, right?

But your head is always on your shoulders, meaning you always carry your thoughts with you. When thoughts are present, voices are present.

What's important to remember is that you're not in danger. There's nobody following you. You're only scared of the CD playing in your head.

Hearing and Seeing What's Not There

The human brain has an area for consciousness. It has other parts, too, for thinking, hearing, seeing, smelling, and the sense of touch.

Sound travels from our ears to the hearing area, then into our consciousness. We then say, "I hear." Seeing an object stimulates the retina in our eyes and the vision area in our brain. Then it goes into our consciousness. We then say, "I see."

Our thinking area may get short-circuited to the seeing area because of the chemical problems of an illness. That short circuiting makes us see what's in our thoughts.

Healthy people dream while sleeping at night. People with a brain disease hallucinate or see things without them being there while they're awake.

In other words, if I'm thinking of a snake and this thought passes through the seeing area of the brain, I will see a snake even if there isn't one. Hallucinations can be frightening.

How can we tell whether the snake is real or a hallucination?

Ask somebody you trust. Point to the snake and ask, "Do you see a snake over there?"

If he jumps and says, "Yes, I see one," that means it's real.

If he says, "I don't see a snake," that means it's a hallucination. Two people have to be able to see or hear for it to be real.

Your mind is playing tricks on you. Ignore the snake the same way you would ignore a rubber snake.

Hurricane in Your Head

Patient: "There are times when my mind gets very troubled. I have these paranoid thoughts. I think the police are after me. They're following me. I think people are watching me and saying bad things about me. I think my company is going to fire me."

Doctor: "A police car was behind you. You pulled over to the side of the road, but to your surprise, the police car just sped by. Has this ever happened to you?"

Patient: "Yes."

Doctor: "You were very sure your boss was going to terminate you, but he didn't. Has this happened to you?"

Patient: "As a matter of fact, not only that. Yesterday, my supervisor and I went to a client. I was 100% sure that they were in cahoots to put me down. The client wasn't going to buy insurance, and I was going to be fired. But he did buy, and my boss said, 'I think you did very well.'"

Doctor: "So, do you recognize that all these thoughts, these voices, sounds, visions, the smell, and the touch are just part of your illness?"

Patient: "Yes, I do. But it's very difficult the moment they attack. I don't know what to say to myself to calm down."

Doctor: "It's simple. You've heard the saying, 'There's a storm in the cup.' In the same way, say, 'There's a hurricane in my head, except that I'm the only one who knows about it. But just like any hurricane, this will also pass.' Be firm in knowing the fact that it's happening only inside your brain. What's going on in there is totally private. No one knows about it. So, in going to any social situation, act normal. Smile, shake hands, talk with people, and nobody will ever know. Keep repeating, 'There's a hurricane inside my head. Just like any hurricane, this will pass, too.'"

Patient: "I'll try. Let's see what happens."

Doctor: "Great. You have succeeded in the past; you will succeed again."

Cars Are Spying On Me

Christopher was very scared when he said, "Doc, I see many cars of the same kind on the road. I surmise that somebody is following me."

I explained to him, "Let's say a person buys a cherry red Honda. Afterwards, he would notice many cherry red Hondas on the road. Why? It's not that more cherry red Hondas fill the highway. They were always there. Other cars on the highway mingled with them. However, the person now becomes sensitive to the other cherry red Hondas because he owns one."

With schizophrenia, the brain of the patient gets very sensitive to things like one make of a car. Others become sensitive to plate numbers that contain certain numbers. In other words, the person becomes very watchful, observant, and suspicious.

In your case, you have started to notice a specific model of a car. The more you watch, the more you see. However, because you're not aware of how your mind works, you will suspect that somebody is spying on you.

Recommended Reading

Aesop, Vernon Jones, V. S., & Rackham, Arthur. (1992).
AESOP'S FABLES (first edition ed.): Avenel Books.

American Psychiatric Association., & American Psychiatric
Association. DSM-5 Task Force. (2013). *Diagnostic and
statistical manual of mental disorders : DSM-5* (5th ed.).
Washington, D.C.: American Psychiatric Association.

Angelo, C. (1981). The Use of Metaphoric Objects in Family
Therapy. *American Journal of Family Therapy, 9*(69-
78).

Bandler, Richard, & Grinder, John. (1979). *Frogs into princes :
neuro linguistic programming.* Moab, Utah: Real People
Press.

Barker, P. (1983). *Basic Child Psychiatry* (4 ed.). London:
Granada, and Baltimore: University Park Press.

Barker, P (1981). Paradoxical Techniques in Psychotherapy. In
D. S. Freeman & B. Trute (Eds.), *Treating Families with
Special Needs.* Ottawa: Canadian Association of Social
Workers.

Bettelheim, Bruno. (1977). *The uses of enchantment : the
meaning and importance of fairy tales.* New York:
Vintage Books.

Burns, George W. (2001). *101 Healing Stories: Using
Metaphors in Therapy* (Ist ed.): John Wiley & Son.

Chalmers, Robert. (2007). *The Jataka* (Vol. 1 & 2): Forgotten Books.

Close, Henry T. (1998). *Metaphor in Psychotherapy: Clinical Applications of Stories and Allegories (Practical Therapist)*: Impact Publishers

Dilts, R., Grinder,J., Bandler,R., Bandler, L.C., & DeLozier,J. (1980). *Neuro-linguistic Programming Volume I.* Cupertino, California: Meta Publications.

Erickson, M. H. (1980a). *Hypnotic Alteration of Sensory, Perceptual and Psychological Processes.* New York: Irivington.

Erickson, M. H. (1980b). *Hypnotic Investigation of Psychodynamic Processes.* New York: Irivington.

Erickson, M. H. (1980c). *Innovative Psychotherapy.* New York: Iriivngton.

Erickson, M. H. (1980d). *A Teaching Seminar with Milton H. Erickson, M.D.* New York: Brunner/Mazel.

Erickson, M. H. . (1980). *The Nature of Hypnosis and Suggestion.* New York: Irvington.

Erickson, M. H., Rossi, E.L.,& Rossi, S. I. (1976). *Hypnotic Realities.* New York: Irvington.

Geary, J.(2009). I Is an Other: The Secret Life of Metaphor and How it Shapes the Way We See the World Kindle Edition HarperCollins e-books

Gordon, D. . (1978). *Therapeutic Metaphors.* Cupertino, California: Meta Publications.

Haley, J. (1973). *Uncommon Therapy: The Psychiatric Techniques of Milton H. Erickson, M.D.* New York: Norton.

Haley, J. (1976). *Problem-Solving Therapy.* San Francisco: Jossey-Bass.

Johnson, Spencer. (1998). *Who moved my cheese? : an amazing way to deal with change in your work and in your life.* New York: Putnam.

John Pollack, J. (2014). Shortcut: How Analogies Reveal Connections, Spark Innovation, and Sell Our Greatest Ideas Kindle Edition Gotham

Lakoff, G. (1980).   Metaphors We Live By (Kindle Edition) University of Chicago Press.

Kopp, Richard R. (1995)). *Metaphor Therapy: Using Client Generated Metaphors In Psychotherapy* Routledge.

Rosen, S. (Ed.). (1982). *My Voice Will Go With You:The Teaching Tales of Milton H. Erickson, M.D.* New York: Norton.

Siegelman, Ellen Y. (1993). *Metaphor and Meaning in Psychotherapy*

Toddard, J.A., Niloofar,A.(2014). *The Big Book of ACT Metaphors: A Practitioner's Guide to Experiential Exercises and Metaphors in Acceptance and Commitment Therapy(, 2014).* New Harbinger Publications. The Guilford Press

Tay, Dennis. (2013). Metaphor in Psychotherapy: A descriptive and prescriptive analysis (Metaphor in Language,

Cognition, and Communication) (pp. 219): John Benjamins Publishing Company.

Turbayne, C. M. (1970). *The Myth of Metaphor*. Columbia, South Carolina: University of South Carolina Press.

Zeig, J. (1980). *In M. H. Erickson, A Teaching Seminar With Milton H. Erickson, M. D.* New York: Brunner/Mazel.

Internet Resources

Cognitive Behaviour Therapy Self-Help Resources
www.getselfhelp.co.uk/freedownloads.htm

Mastering the Metaphor, ACBS World Conference IX, Colleen Ehrnstrom, Ph.D., Boulder
https://contextualscience.org/system/files/Mastering_The_Metaphor_Ehrnstrom.pdf
Colorado, USA
http://contextualscience.org/system/files/Mastering_The_Metaphor_Ehrn

Daniel Eckstein—Six Types of Counseling Metaphors
www.alfredadler.org

Metaphors in the Therapeutic Encounter—Cruse Bereavement Care
http://www.cruse.org.uk/conference

Psychology Tools
http://www.psychologytools.org/metaphor.html

Therapeutic Metaphor
http://www.therapeuticmetaphors.com

Visual Metaphors—Accept and Change
http://www.acceptandchange.com/visual-metaphors

The place to find metaphors for therapy and therapeutic short stories, videos, and audio. How to write a metaphor.
http://www.therapymetaphors.com/

Metaphor Therapy
https://www.youtube.com/watch?v=ev3RYZOyZjA

Storytelling & Metaphor in Therapy—Part 1 James Hazlerig & Richard Nongard on YouTube
www.youtube.com/watch?v=_istOGRablo

Passengers on a Bus—An Acceptance & Commitment Therapy (ACT) Metaphor
https://www.youtube.com/watch?v=Z29ptSuoWRc

YouTube Videos from *Metaphors of Healing* by Harish Malhotra. They are called Helpful Hints for Hang-ups.
https://www.youtube.com/user/nanabhai

On YouTube
https://www.youtube.com/watch?v=ev3RYZOvZjA
www.youtube.com/watch?v=uDkEEpC-73g
www.youtube.com/watch?v=uDkEEpC-73g
https://www.youtube.com/watch?v=pYjIYB-yT9c
https://www.youtube.com/watch?v=dcfZFURoH0s
https://www.youtube.com/watch?v=q2TI6z0mxg8
https://www.youtube.com/watch?v=vOrxiHmoijw
https://www.youtube.com/watch?v=LV4DGkPc-eA
https://www.youtube.com/watch?v=Uc4YcqxTWkI
https://www.youtube.com/watch?v=IHU2HzqJgvA
https://www.youtube.com/watch?v=dB8MnPjmQOs

Index

mules, 138

multibit screwdrivers, 54–55

NA. *See* Narcotics Anonymous

narcotics. *See* addiction

Narcotics Anonymous (NA), 190, 275

natural living philosophy, 76

negative thoughts, 171

nitpicking, 258–59

noise, ineffective, 251

non-responders, 222–23

nonsense, 46

Norris, W. E., 62

nose and ear cleaning, 225

obsessive-compulsive disorder (OCD), 257, 258–59

office squabbles, 133

openness, 51, 105–6, 224

operations, 173–74

opportunities, 77

Other Books by Harish Malhotra

Metaphors of Healing: Playful Language in Psychotherapy and Everyday Life, Hamilton Books 2014 (Available on Amazon)

Pathways to Hope: Innovative Insights for Therapists and Patients, Hamilton Books 2014 (Available on Amazon)

About the Author

Harish K. Malhotra, MD is a board certified psychiatrist in private practice in Summit, NJ. He was born in Lahore, now Pakistan, to Krishna and Sohan Lal. The family moved to India and his father worked in several different cities. Dr. Malhotra finished his MBBS (the MD equivalent) from Government Medical College, Amritsar. He did his residency in psychiatry at the Post Graduate Institute in Chandigarh. He came to the United States in 1973 and completed his residency in psychiatry from The University of Medicine and Dentistry in Newark, NJ in 1975. He is a clinical associate professor of psychiatry at Rutgers University as well as the past Chairman of the Department of Psychiatry at Overlook Medical Center in Summit, NJ.

Dr. Malhotra has had over 20 articles published in scientific journals. *Metaphors of Healing: Playful Language in Psychotherapy and Everyday Life* is his first book and made the bestseller list for Hamilton Books. His second book, *Pathways to Hope: Innovative Insights for Therapists and Patients* is also available on Amazon.com.

See his funny videos based on the metaphors:
https://www.youtube.com/user/nanabhai/videos